MW01452195

Letters from Your Children

Letters from Your Children

A Wake-Up Call for Parents

Officer J. A. Babb

VANTAGE PRESS
New York

FIRST EDITION

All rights reserved, including the right of
reproduction in whole or in part in any form.

Copyright © 1997 by Officer J. A. Babb

Published by Vantage Press, Inc.
516 West 34th Street, New York, New York 10001

Manufactured in the United States of America
ISBN: 0-533-11985-5

Library of Congress Catalog No.: 96-90274

0 9 8 7 6 5 4 3 2 1

To the true love of my life,
my precious daughter,
Brittaney Elan,
and
to all of my students

Contents

Preface ix
Acknowledgments xi
Introduction xv

1. "It Takes an Entire Village..." 1
2. To the Parents 5
3. The "Question Box" 10
4. A Letter from Caitlin 13
5. Letters from Jessica 17
6. Letters from "Anonymous" 21
7. A Letter from a Stepfather 29
8. Letters from Allison 33
9. Letters from Katie 37
10. A Letter from David 40
11. Letters from a Gangster's Girlfriend 43
12. More Letters from "Anonymous" 47
13. Letters from Stephanie 57
14. Letters from Diana 60
15. Letters from a "White Girl" 64
16. Letters from Maggie and Her Mother 69
17. Letters from Stephan and Tamara 73
18. Letters from Brittaney 76
19. Even More Letters from "Anonymous" 82
20. Responding to the "Toughies" 87
21. Who Made Me an Expert? 98
22. The Search for Understanding 101
23. The Hidden Meaning 106
24. A Child's Feelings; A Child's Right 112

25.	Is Your Child "at Risk"?	115
26.	Jason's Story	117
27.	Fulfilling Your Child's Needs	125
28.	Divorce: From a Child's Perspective	128
29.	Helpful Hints for Parents	138
30.	An Afterthought	142
31.	To the Critics	145
32.	My Next Project	149

References 151

Preface

This book is my **gift** to the **parents**;
   my **duty** to the **children**;
      my **contribution** to the **"village."**

Acknowledgments

This is the section of the book that I least looked forward to writing. I would love to acknowledge all of the special people who have supported my endeavors and assisted in making this book possible.

However, having worked with more than three hundred educators and 25,000 students, I fear that the completed list would be nearly as long as the text itself. By far my greatest fear is that, by attempting to acknowledge a few, I may be perceived as minimizing the efforts of many others. Inevitably I will leave someone out. However, I will attempt to acknowledge as many as possible, while offending as few as possible.

I will begin by expressing my sincere appreciation to the most important contributors of all, my students. There is a philosophy in the law-enforcement profession that the best way to catch a criminal is to be able to think like a criminal. The best investigators in the world all have one major quality in common. They have achieved an understanding of the criminal mind. They have done this by allowing themselves to become students while allowing the criminal to become their teacher. It is the application of this generic philosophy, to teaching, that has enabled me to enjoy the level of success that I have with my students. **(This is by no means an attempt to compare my students to criminals.)** It is through listening to my students that I have learned to effectively communicate with them and to understand the pressures and emotions that they experience. **While each and every one of my students collectively assisted me in the learning process, it would not be feasible to list all twenty-five thousand of them.** However, there have been several students who, over the years, have gone above and beyond with "the education of Officer Babb." It is through their openness, their honesty, and their trust, as well as their willingness to share their thoughts, feelings, fears, and concerns that the following students have not only contributed to my success with children but inspired me to write *Letters from Your Children*. I would like to thank:

Elan ("S.W.")	Amy H.	Gina ("Slick")
Liana	Justin	Nadia
Josh	Kelli	Misty
Claudia	Meagan	Carri
Courtney	Heath	Melissa
Aaron	Chris	Patricia
Lindsay	Becky	?

The next group to which I would like to express my heartfelt appreciation are those dedicated women and men who have taken on the responsibility of educating, mentoring, and counseling our nation's children and preparing them to be good citizens, as well as productive members of the human community. It is my sincere belief that the role of "educator" has become the single most critical role in contemporary society. These educators literally mold the future of our world far beyond their own mortal existence. In recent decades these unsung heroes have, in addition to educating our children, been given the task of taking up the parenting slack, which has been caused by the rapidly deteriorating American family. During the past five years, I have had the opportunity to work with more than three hundred educators from five different school districts. While I have acquired invaluable information and experience from observing each of them, there are two particular educators to whom I owe a special debt of gratitude. I would like to thank Kathy Forrester and Mary Neskora for serving as my most dedicated mentors and for being so selfless in sharing the very special gift that they possess for working with and motivating young minds.

I would like to express my gratitude to Mike Knox (author: *Gangsta in the House;* Momentum Books Ltd.), not only for his guidance and support during my years as a rookie patrol officer, but also for his valuable advice on how to get my first book published. I would also like to express my appreciation to Bryce and Kerri for their critical review of my original manuscript, from a parent's perspective. This section would not be complete without acknowledging Patricia Paetow and Dr. Lydia Long for the patience, the encouragement and the support that they have provided me. Finally, I would like to once again thank the most important contributors of all, my students. Words cannot express what they have added to my life. Should **Letters from Your Children** ever realize a profit, a portion of that profit will be invested in our nation's most valuable resource, the children. Anticipating the curiosity of my students, I must add that none of the letters that appear in this text were contributed by the students whose names appear in the "Acknowledgments" section.

Introduction

As a police officer and DARE instructor with the Houston Police Department, I have taught more than 25,000 elementary and middle-school students. I currently teach the seventeen-lesson DARE (Drug Abuse Resistance Education) curriculum in four major school districts. In addition to classroom instruction, I visit with the children during lunch and recess. During the four-month program, the students and I become close friends. As I have earned their trust, many of the students come to me seeking advice regarding personal problems and concerns with which they are trying to cope. In addition to receiving personal counseling, the children also contribute *anonymous* questions and letters, to the Question Box, which will be explained in chapter 2. Under the protection of anonymity, which will be continued throughout this text, the children share personal problems and concerns that they would otherwise be very hesitant to share, even with their parents. Although the primary focus of the DARE program is to teach children how to resist pressures to become involved in drugs and gangs, many of the children use the program as a means of learning how to deal with other pressures in their life.

As a parent and DARE instructor, it terrifies me to realize the pressures that these children try to deal with on their own, pressures of which their parents are rarely made aware until, in some cases, it is too late. Too many times I have had the sad task of informing parents that their child has become a victim of drug abuse, gang violence, or some other tragedy. In many cases, these are wonderful parents with excellent parenting skills who are shocked to discover that their child had ever been exposed to any of these hazards.

In *Letters from Your Children: A Wake-Up Call for Parents,* parents will be able to read sample letters and questions that have been received from their children. The letters have only been modified to the degree necessary to ensure the anonymity of the students. While a majority of the letters are from elementary students, several of them are from middle-school students who have kept in touch by mail. *Letters from Your Children* offers tremendous insight into the many pressures to which your child may be exposed. I hope that you will find this information helpful, not only in understanding and preparing your child to deal with these additional pressures, but also in enhancing the communication between you and your child regarding their hidden concerns.

Letters from Your Children

Chapter 1
"It Takes an Entire Village . . ."

It was early one morning when I entered the classroom for the first time at a particular school. Eager to make a good first impression, I had spent much of the early morning hours preparing my lesson. As I caught my first glance of the students, I could not help but ponder that haunting question that had stolen so much of my sleep the night before. Will this be the wonderful "class from Heaven" or the infamous "class from . . ." (I'm sure you get the point). Following a brief introduction, the teacher returned to her desk, releasing the class to me.

Although the class numbered more than twenty, it was one particular student who immediately caught my attention. Noticeably taller than his classmates, he sat quietly, with an intimidating aura about him. He wore a sullied, off-white T-shirt, which displayed the emblem of a favored sports team. The T-shirt was complemented by a faded blue jean jacket and jeans, which were only visible from the knees down. He had light-colored hair, which I'm almost certain had been washed at least once that week.

As I began to address the class for the first time, the student rose suddenly from his seat. Fearing that he was going for his weapon, I watched closely as he turned his desk around to the back of the room. He then returned to his seat. As I stood alone in the front of the room looking at twenty-four faces and the back of one head, I glanced toward the teacher, hoping for a clue as to what actions I should take. However, she had no significant reaction to the trauma that I was now experiencing. Taking her lack of reaction as a vote of confidence, I was determined to complete the lesson as if nothing unusual had occurred.

Once the lesson had been completed and the students were on their way to lunch, I asked the teacher for an explanation as well as some helpful advice. The teacher informed me that the student ("David") was oppositional (quite literally, I'd say). She said that he had been that way since coming to the school. Although many had tried, there had been little success in getting through to him. She had found it best not to pressure him to conform with the class but to let the specialists work with him. However, she said, "If you like a challenge, here is your opportunity." This motivated me!

Prior to class the following week, I asked the teacher to send David on a short errand. This would give me an opportunity to speak to the class without him being present. As expected, when I entered the room, David turned his desk around to where it faced the back of the room. Honoring my previous request, the teacher sent him on a short errand to another teacher's room.

During his brief absence, I instructed all of the students to turn their desks around so that they were facing the back of the room. I then told the students that in the future any time David turned his desk around, they were to do the same and continue the lesson as if nothing unusual had occurred. If any of the students were asked by David for an explanation, they were to respond by saying, "Think about it."

David returned to the classroom to find the entire class facing the back of the room from which I was teaching. Following a brief hesitation, David returned to his seat, being careful not to show any reaction to what was happening.

Following the lesson, I decided to spend lunch with the fifth-grade students. Upon entering the lunchroom, I noticed David sitting alone at a table, which was set off from the rest of the tables. After several of my ill-fated attempts to initiate a dialogue, David finally looked up and asked, "Man, why are you messing with me?" I simply responded by saying, **"Think about it."**

Once again, the following week David stood and turned his desk around. This time, however, the entire class stood with him and turned their desks in the same direction, toward the back wall. With a partial grin on his face, David paused and mumbled to the class, "Man, why are you all messing with me?" The entire class responded by saying, **"Think about it!"** From the back of the room, I continued my lesson.

The following week David entered the classroom to discover his classmates lined up along the walls, waiting to see which way he would face his desk. David broke into laughter as he strutted over to his desk. As he turned his desk around, the rest of the class did the same.

Once again, I sat at David's table during lunch. This time, however, we were joined by several other students. Although he did not dominate the conversation, David did begin to open up and interact with the other students.

During the following weeks, a new David began to emerge, the real David in my opinion. David began showing up to school nicely dressed and well groomed. His participation in class increased, as did his interaction with classmates outside of class. Perhaps the most telling sign as to the true influence of the course on David was the crush that he developed on Rachael, a beautiful, outgoing honor student who had asked him to be her partner in one of our class projects.

Following our DARE graduation several months later, David reminded me before I left school that day to check my box, which was located inside the school office. Upon checking my box, I found a brief, unsigned note. The note read: **"I thought about it. Thanks."**

The last news I received regarding David was that he had moved out of the state with his mother and his new stepfather. Rachael and David were still pen pals.

I chose to share this story in order to set forth a very sincere belief that I hold: that every child on this earth is capable of being reached in some way by someone. I did receive a minimal degree of criticism for the way I chose to reach David. However, it sometimes requires that unconventional measures be taken to finally reach a child like David. It could just as easily have been a counselor, a coach, an extended family member, or another teacher who finally discovered a way to reach David. The important thing is that someone managed to get through to him. I will be the first to admit that luck played a significant role in *our* success with David. However, with such an abundance of bad luck around, why argue when a little good luck comes our way. There are many more Davids in this world waiting to be reached.

I have often heard the old African proverb, "It takes an entire village to raise a single child." Although the village is much larger now, the saying still holds true today. The village is now comprised of parents, grandparents, teachers, coaches, counselors, police officers, doctors, dentists, babysitters, and many more. It will definitely take all of us working together to raise each child. As I mentioned earlier, this book is **my contribution to the "village."**

Chapter 2
To the Parents

Please understand that this text is not intended to criticize parents. It is not my place, nor am I in any position to be critical of others' parenting skills. Rather, it is the intent of *Letters from Your Children* to share information, as well as my own observations, with parents and to enhance their own awareness of the many hidden pressures and concerns that are being experienced by their children. As a parent myself, I have come to realize that parenting is a continual learning process. Much of the knowledge and many of the parenting skills are gained from experience. Since every child is different, I feel that it is imperative for parents to share the knowledge that they have acquired from their own unique parenting experience. I have observed and interacted with your children in a wide range of settings.

As a DARE instructor, I have interacted with your children in the classroom, in the lunchroom and on the playground. As a patrol officer, I have observed these same children when they are away from their parents and teachers. I have seen firsthand the pressure situations in which these children become involved, many times inadvertently. In the following pages, I will attempt to share those observations. Parenting has changed in recent years and will continue to do so. In contemporary society, a parent can do all the right things and still have difficulties.

It is my sincere hope that this text will in some way aid parents as they face the most challenging job of our day, that of being a parent.

I would be remiss in pretending that many of these parents would not be horrified to discover that their children have shared some of the intimate information that you will soon be reading. However, what should be more disconcerting is why they chose to share it with someone other than one of their parents. The truth is that these children had an intense need to share these concerns. Had it not been me with whom they chose to share them, it would have been someone else. Among my primary goals in writing this text is to increase the chances that the child's parent will be that *"someone else"* with whom they share their future concerns. Additionally, there are four very important objectives that I hope to achieve by the time the reader completes the final chapter of this book.

These four objectives are:

1. To help parents realize the importance of creating an environment in which their children will be encouraged to share, and feel comfortable in sharing their concerns.
2. To assist parents in creating such an environment.
3. To help "all concerned" to realize the importance of having appropriate outlets available for those children who may not have a family environment that is conducive to venting their most intimate concerns.
4. To help facilitate effective communication between parents and their children. (I consider this fourth objective to be so vital in the parent-

child relationship that I have devoted several chapters to this particular issue.)

Please take comfort in knowing that my primary consideration in writing this book was to ensure the anonymity of the children and their families. My original idea for this book was to publish the actual letters (with parent's and child's permission of course) and block out the child's name as well as other key information. This was to have a more profound effect on the reader as well as to add to the authenticity of the letters. However, I feared the remote chance that someone might be able to identify a child upon viewing the letter and recognizing the handwriting.

I ultimately decided upon this format because it allowed the book to be written while ensuring the anonymity of the children, the parents and the schools. The fears, the feelings, and the concerns expressed in the letters that you will soon be reading are from actual students. While many of the letters are accompanied by my own response to the student or parent, some of the letters "speak for themselves" and required no response. The latter few letters were included for the sole reason of alerting parents to the existence of that particular scenario.

The letters that have been included in this text were chosen because they are indicative of common concerns and scenarios which have been shared or expressed by numerous students. If, as you are reading a particular letter, the scenario appears to be similar to one that exists within your own family, please allow me to offer a way of coping with the initial feeling of trepidation. Rather than thinking, "Oh my gosh, this letter is from my child," you might simply think, "Oh, so we are not the only family that experiences these problems." Whether or not you can relate to the scenarios which are mentioned in these letters, it is important to realize that no child is immune from becoming involved in any of these situations, not even yours.

The first step in protecting your child is to recognize that these scenarios do exist and take steps to prepare our children for coping with such pressures.

Several of these letters were contributed from officers throughout the country. Any letters that involved concerns or scenarios of a unique nature were not included. This was out of concern that the uniqueness of the situation could possibly compromise the anonymity of the child, parent, or school. While several of the letters are accompanied by comments "From the author," chapters 21-30 address more specifically the issues that are raised in the letters. Keeping the following "Important Points" in mind, I hope you will find this text to be informing, entertaining and worth your investment of time and money. For those parents who, after reading these letters, feel as though you have just gotten away with reading your kid's diary, *shame on you!*

Important Points

While reading *Letters From Your Children,* it will be important to keep the following points in mind.

- The letters and questions that you are about to read were contributed by students who range in age from nine to fourteen years.
- While many of the letters were contributed by myself, additional letters were contributed by other officers as well.

- Key information has been modified or paraphrased only to the degree necessary to guarantee the anonymity of the students.
- Students are always informed that any information received that revealed a possible threat to the safety and well-being of any student would be promptly acted upon by the appropriate official or agency.
- The students were always strongly encouraged to discuss their concerns further with their parents.
- In some cases, the students are also referred to the school counselor.
- Prior to the culmination of a class or program, my mailing address (P.O. box) is displayed in the classroom. The students are encouraged to keep in touch, but only with the permission and knowledge of their parents.
- Upon answering each letter, the envelope is conspicuously marked and addressed to ensure that the parents are aware of the correspondence.
- The information in this text is not meant to represent the opinions, policies, or the accepted practices of the Houston Police Department, any school district, any DARE organization, or any of their members. Furthermore, this book has not been endorsed by any of the previously listed individuals, agencies or organizations.

Chapter 3
The "Question Box"

The **"Question Box"** (usually a simple decorated shoebox) is placed in a location that is conveniently accessible to the students within a particular classroom. The students are encouraged to contribute questions and statements to the **"Question Box"** regarding drugs, gangs, peer pressure, and any problems or concerns that they may be experiencing. The students are asked to decorate the box and choose where it will be located. A portion of each lesson or presentation is dedicated to responding to questions and statements from the **"Question Box."** The rules governing the **"Question Box"** are as follows:*

- It is preferred that questions and statements be anonymous. This guideline is strongly emphasized and consistently reinforced.
- Avoid using names or titles when sharing personal experiences that involve classmates or family members (i.e., "I know someone that gets drunk every weekend" rather than "Brianna Doe gets drunk every weekend").
- The **"Question Box"** is *not* to be used for snitch-

*Denotes rules and instructions that are also set forth in the "THE DARE BOX" section (p. xi) of the official DARE America curriculum.

ing. Such use will constitute abuse of the **"Question Box,"** unless of course the information is regarding an imminent threat to the safety and well-being of another.
- Questions of interest to all students will be read aloud to the class.
- No "put-downs" or inappropriate language.
- **No student should ever enter or extract anything from the "Question Box" for any reason.**
- Anonymity will only be compromised out of concern for the safety and well-being of a student.

The **"Question Box"** serves a vital role in the classroom. Under the protection of anonymity, the students share concerns that they would otherwise hesitate to share even with their parents. Although anonymity is strongly encouraged, students will occasionally identify themselves when contributing letters or questions of a more personal or serious nature or when requesting a nonpublic conference. This is usually out of concern that their classmates will be able to discover their identity when the question is read aloud. Prior to offering my response to the question or statement, I will often elicit responses from other students. In addition to having a respected authority figure respond, the student has an opportunity to hear how his/her peers would deal with the same situation. I have not yet achieved an adequate understanding of what I call the **"Question Box Phenomenon."** However, I will share it in hopes that the reader may be able to figure it out. Occasionally, students will place notes in the **"Question Box"** in which they reveal a particular concern or event that has occurred in their lives; however, such a student neither identifies himself nor asks for any advice regarding the matter. I guess, to some small degree, the student experiences a sense of relief just knowing that someone else is aware of the problem without risking the possible consequences that come with being identified. It has been my experience that the students not only appreciate the **"Question Box"** but eagerly await and participate in that portion of each lesson. Although by different names, I have seen variations of the "Question Box" in several classrooms that I have visited. I have used the "Question Box" for several years. Whether it is called the "Question Box," the "Suggestion Box," the "Help Box," the "DARE Box," or the "Advice Box," no class should be without one.

Chapter 4
A Letter from Caitlin

Letter 1

Dear Officer Babb,

Sorry that I haven't written in a while. I have been really busy with school. Seventh grade is fun, so far. I finally have a boyfriend. He is in the ninth grade. I am the only seventh grader with a boyfriend in the ninth grade. A lot of my friends have boyfriends in the eighth grade. Anyway, I have sort of a problem that I need to talk to you about.

My boyfriend and his old girlfriend used to have sex. We haven't done it yet, but I think he is going to want us to do it later. I don't mind kissing and ***doing the other stuff,** but I don't want to have sex until I'm married. I'm afraid that if we don't do it, he will eventually break up. What do you think I should do? I don't want to lose him, but I don't want to have sex yet. Can you please write me soon and help me.

Sincerely,
Caitlin

From the Author

*I chose to eliminate part of the second paragraph in a effort to spare parents the stress.

When these girls first reach middle school, it's a sign of prestige to have an upper-grade-level boyfriend. You can bet that some of the upper-grade-level boys attempt to exploit this trend.

This particular girl is an excellent student, who comes from an upper-middle-class family. She enjoys gymnastics and reading romance novels. She has a very conservative value system and is a hopeless romantic. Although I did offer some guidance, she ultimately consulted with her older sister as well. She was afraid to talk to her parents out of fear that she would disappoint her father. She lives for her daddy's approval.

Response

Dear Caitlin,

It's about time! I was beginning to think that you had forgotten all about me. It sounds like you have a tough dilemma. At least that's one way of looking at it. However, there is another way of looking at it. It could be your boyfriend who has the tough dilemma. There are at least two ways of looking at the situation.

You feel fortunate to have a boyfriend who is in the ninth grade. You care for him. You may even feel as though you are in love with him. You think he is cool and you enjoy the prestige that comes with having an older boyfriend, especially one who is two grades ahead of you. Since he is older and more experienced, you feel that there are sacrifices that you will have to make in order to keep him. Taking on the responsibilities, as well as the possible consequences, of becoming sexually active are just a few of the sacrifices that you feel must be made if you want to keep an older boyfriend. It comes with the territory. This is one way of looking at it. However, there is another way of looking at it.

Most girls who are your age feel the same way you do about becoming sexually active. Most will wait until much later in life to become active. Many, who decide to wait until they are married, are strong enough and secure enough to wait. Therefore, if he truly cares for you and wants to keep you, your boyfriend has a tough dilemma. He needs to realize that respecting your decisions and values, and having to wait for as long as is necessary are just a few of the sacrifices that he will have to make if he intends to keep a special girl like you as his girlfriend. It comes with the territory.

Some important decisions need to be made. You have already made your decision a long time ago. You have spent your life honoring that decision. Now your boyfriend has an important decision to make. One of those decisions will be whether he can honor the decision that you have made. Remember! It is only right when both of you are ready. At this point, only one of you is ready, or believes that he is. You have a long life ahead of you. You are a wonderful girl and will have plenty of opportunities to find a wonderful guy. When you do find him, you will have saved a special part of you for him. That can only be your decision to make. I have confidence in you.

I guess I'll go for now. Let me know how things work out. Take care and keep in touch.

Your friend,
Officer Babb

Final note

Caitlin eventually discovered that her boyfriend was also seeing a girl who attended another school. They are no longer together.

Chapter 5
Letters from Jessica

Letter 1

Dear Officer Babb,
    I got to tell you something. You see my dad drinks a lot. He sometimes gets drunk. He not too long ago had hepatitis. You know the sickness that affects your liver. Well, it was because of his drinking and that didn't stop him from drinking. I don't know how to get him to stop. My parents are divorced and I see my dad every other weekend. I would probably hurt him if I told him that I never wanted *(to)* see him again. But I do kind of. I love my dad but if he keeps drinking he can get really sick. I don't want to see him get sick again. He gets irritated when I try to talk to him and never lets me finish. Please tell me how to get him to stop.

Sincerely,
Jessica

    P.S. Sorry for the mis-spells.

Letter 2

Dear Officer Babb,
    I took your advice and wrote a letter to my dad, saying how I feel. I told him that I love him a lot and I want him

to live long enough to meet my future husband and know his grandchildren. I told him that I was afraid that if he kept on drinking that he may not live to do those things. He called mom and asked if he could have me for the weekend . We talked a lot. It was really neat and a little weird at first. He said he would drink less from now on.

Sincerely,
Jessica

Letter 3

Dear Officer Babb,

    I have bad news and good news. I will give you the bad news first. My dad wanted to see me this weekend, but since my mom let him see me last weekend, she said "no." My dad got real mad and they argued on the phone. I talked my mom into letting me go if I found someone to take me to his house. She doesn't like for me to drive with him.

    When I got to my dad's house he was drunk in front of the TV. He asked me to get him a beer. I was real mad, so I went to the kitchen and took all of his beer out of the refrigerator. I opened some of the cans and started pouring the beer out into the sink. He didn't like that much. He got real mad and started to hit me, but I knew he wouldn't. I told him "You can hit me instead of drinking, if that's what it takes you to stop drinking." He started crying and said that he would never hurt me. I told him that he has been hurting me and he has to stop. He helped me pour the rest of the beer out. I think he will make it this time because he said that he loves me and he is proud of me. He's never said that stuff before. I love him now so much.

Sincerely,
Jessica

P.S. Sometimes I feel like I'm the parent and my dad is the child.

P.S.S. Thank you for helping me all of these weeks.

Letter 4

Dear Officer Babb,

Not much has happened since the last time that we talked. I think my dad is still doing OK. I know he needs help to really get better, so I have been trying to see him and talk to him more. I leave a message on his answering machine every day when I get home from school. I can't call him on the weekend though, because my mom gets mad, unless it is my weekend to see him. My mom doesn't like me helping him so much.

We had an argument the other day because my mom thinks that I worry to much about my dad. I told her that just because she stopped loving him doesn't mean that I have to stop loving him. We stopped arguing for a little while, so she could go to the store and get some more cigarettes. I think she just wanted to get away for a little while, so she could think about what she was going to say to me next. I can always tell when she's not sure about what to say to me. When she got back we started arguing again. She said that she didn't stop loving him. She just lost respect for him because of what he was doing to his self and our family. She said that the reason we left him was because she didn't want me to watch my own father gradually kill his self with alcohol. I guess it is OK for me to watch her gradually kill her self with cigarettes. Don't worry, I didn't say that to her. I'm not that crazy yet. I think that our argument helped a little, because tonight she asked me if I was going to call my dad. I love my mom a lot, but sometimes she can be a little difficult. That's also what she says about me.

I am going to miss talking to you after we graduate. I told my mom that you have helped me a lot and I asked her if it would be OK for you and me to keep in touch. We could be like Pen Pals. She said that she would think about it. I think she's afraid that I will tell you to much personal. But I have to talk to someone and you are always good at listening to me. I guess I'll go for now.

Sincerely,
Jessica

From the Author: Regarding Jessica

Jessica is twelve years old, going on thirty. She is currently living with her mother, in a lower-middle-class environment. She is extremely bright and very analytical, as you may have gathered from reading her letters.

Jessica is a very nurturing and outgoing person. Although she gets along well with her peers, she has few close friends who are her own age. She relates to people on an adult level and has an expectation that others will do the same when interacting with her. As you may imagine this trait has, on occasion, caused her to butt heads with the authority figures in her life; this has included me.

I still receive an occasional letter from Jessica. Her father continues to do well. Her mother has become more understanding of Jessica's concerns for her father. She has also agreed to accompany Jessica to one of her father's support group meetings.

Chapter 6
Letters from "Anonymous"

Anonymous Student

Dear Officer Babb,
    I am really worried about my little brother. He is nine years old. He use to play around with the scented markers. You know the ones that are OK for kids to smell. He now smells real magic markers. Just like the ones you talked about during our lesson on inhalants. He's been trying to get me and my friend to smell them also. He says that they calm him down when he's under stress.
    I don't know what to do. Me and my brother have been getting along better lately and are becoming like friends. If I tell my parents, I am afraid that he will think I have violated our trust or something.
    I told him what using inhalants can do to him. I also told him about the film you showed us and the stories that you told. He says that I should be glad that he doesn't do drugs.

One of your students,

    P.S. Can you please read this to the class, like you do sometimes and ask what the other students would do.

From the Author

For obvious reasons, this letter **GREATLY** concerned me. After reading the letter to the class, I placed it inside my briefcase. I had intended on having the teacher try to identify the handwriting, so that I could actually speak with the student. However, after returning from lunch, having left my briefcase in the classroom, I found the letter had mysteriously disappeared from my briefcase.

Realizing that her nine-year-old brother (acting on a hunch that the letter had been written by a female student) could have been in either the third or the fourth grade, I decided to present a lesson on *The Possible Consequences of Using Inhalants* to the third- and fourth-grade students. During the third-grade lesson, one particular student continually had his hand up to ask questions. In the forty-five-minute lesson, he asked thirteen questions, all regarding the use of inhalants. **(Hello!!!)** I had previously asked the teachers to identify any male student who had a sister in my fifth-grade class. There was only one student. You guessed it; the inquisitive third grader.

His teacher had recently become concerned about him due to "a dramatic change in his personality and his appearance." The teacher said that he used to be well groomed, energetic, and very sociable. Recently, according to the teacher, his appearance and behavior had both changed dramatically. His appearance had become sloppy. He had dark rings under his eyes and had become less sociable with the other students. **(Hello!!!** In case you missed the last clue.)

Later that day I requested a private conference with the fifth-grade sister. During our conference, my directness was reciprocated by my fifth-grade student. Our

conference was very pleasant and very positive. However, the student insisted that she had not written the note and that her brother did not use inhalants. The following week, I found a letter in the "Question Box" that read:
> Thank you!
> for helping me with my brother

Talk about playing "head games"!

Without giving out too much information, I will say this student comes from an upper-middle-class family, where she lives with her younger brother and older sister. Although she is somewhat introverted in school, I found this student to be extremely intelligent and very witty. I still receive letters from her occasionally.

Anonymous Student

Dear Officer ———,

We have a lake house that we spend time at on some weekends and during the summer. Last weekend we took our neighbors to the lake house with us. They have three kids also. During the daytime, we take one of our boats out and do water activities, like skiing and boogie-boarding. At night time, the grownups sit around and drink and the kids find other stuff to do. We got permission to set up a tent near the boat house and camp out for the night.

One of the neighbor's sons brought a can of butane, like the stuff that kid used in the movie that you showed us. He sprayed some of it in a plastic bag and put it up to his mouth to inhale. After a little while, he started feeling really good so we all tried it. It didn't make me feel good though. I got a little sick at my stomach. He wanted to do it again the next night, but we didn't want to. He went outside by his self and did it. When he came back in, it smelled inside the house. My parents started to check to see if we had a gas leak inside the house. Me and my brother only did it once. My chest hurt real bad for couple of days after we did it, but it feels better now. Will it hurt us, even if we don't ever do it again?

One of your students,

P.S. Can you please answer this today.

From the Author

Use of inhalants is at an epidemic level with today's children. I feel this is due in part to three reasons:

1. Inhalants ("the poor man's drug") are inexpensive and extremely accessible to children. Butane, paint, shoe polish, permanent markers, glue, etc., are common household items that are used by some children to get high.
2. Many students do not consider using inhalants as abusing drugs.
3. Many parents are in DENIAL.

These students attend a prestigious public school, which is located in a relatively affluent community. Many members of the faculty, as well as a small faction of parents, feel that their children do not need special programs, such as DARE, GREAT, and similar programs. This is not the only school at which I have heard this sentiment expressed. Some of them will, no doubt, attempt to discredit this text. DENIAL is at an epidemic level in many of these communities. Thus, when one of their children becomes a victim of drugs or gangs they are dumbfounded. There is then a rush to place blame; anywhere but where it belongs.

A Quickly Related Story

I recently heard of a tragedy involving the daughter of a schoolteacher. This teacher's daughter (we will call her Allison) was a wonderful girl. She was an excellent student and had never become involved in drugs or gangs. Allison's best friend used inhalants. She would inhale butane several times each month. This girl had been pressuring Allison to inhale with her. Fortunately Allison had been able to resist the pressure.

One time Allison and her friend were spending the night at a friend's slumber party. Allison's friend had convinced the other girls to get high with her. All but Allison had agreed to inhale butane. Then the pressure was turned on Allison. Here is how the conversation allegedly went:

Allison's friend: "Come on, just try it once to see if you like it. One time is not going to hurt you."
Allison: "I don't know what that stuff will do to me."
Friend: "Listen, I have been doing this stuff for months and I am still here. Try it one time and if you don't like it I'll stop bothering you."

That night Allison inhaled butane for the first time. She died shortly after inhaling the butane, two days short of her thirteenth birthday. I always tell my students that I can't guarantee that they will die the first time they try inhaling; however, no one else can guarantee them that they won't die the first time.

Anonymous Student

Dear Officer ———,
    I have a brother in the fourth grade who likes to drink wine coolers. A couple of times each month, we have a lot of people over for a cookout, at our house. My parents always get big boxes of wine coolers. Our friends nicknamed my brother The Bartender, because he always get the drinks for everyone. During the cookouts, he grabs extra wine coolers and hides them, so him and his friends can drink them during the week. He doesn't share them with his friends anymore. Now he drinks one wine cooler every night, in the bathroom, before he goes to bed. He says that it helps him sleep better. He throws the bottle out of the bathroom window, and picks it up in the morning, when he goes to school. I'm not afraid that he will become an alcoholic on wine coolers, but I am afraid that he might get into trouble, if he keeps drinking.

    P.S. You can read this to the class, since I didn't put my name on it.

Anonymous Student

Dear Officer ———,
    Have you ever heard of the game called Blackout? It's when you stand on you head, while two other people hold your legs in the air. Then they help you get on your feet really fast so you can run toward a wall. The person that gets the closest to the wall, before they blackout wins. My brother and his friends play it sometimes. They usually only blackout for a few seconds, but the other night one of his friends blacked out for a lot longer. Can someone die from playing Blackout?

                                                 Anonymous

Anonymous Student

Dear Officer ———,

My brother is in the eighth grade. Sometimes him and his friends play a game called center line. They drink alcohol or smoke **marijuana** to get high. Then they lay down in the middle of the road and wait for cars to come by. My brother says that the danger gives them a rush. I'm afraid he is going to get hurt or killed. Have you ever heard of kids playing center line.

Sincerely,
A student

Anonymous Student

Dear Officer ———,

Remember me? I have the brother in the eighth grade who plays that game called center line. Last weekend my brother and some of his friends drank beer and played center line. The first person to go, picks where the next person will lay down. My brother laid down in the middle of the road that leads into our neighborhood. The next car to come by was my mom. She got real upset when she found out what he was doing. She never found out that they had been drinking beer though. He got in major trouble anyway.

Sincerely,
A student

From the Author

I was aware of this particular game, although by a different name. However, I had not been aware that my students knew anything about it. I recently had an opportunity to address the issue, following a evening news program that dealt with the story of a teen who had lost his life while playing a similar game. Although many of my students had heard of the game, none admitted to having ever played the game. Most thought it was an asinine game.

Chapter 7
A Letter from a Stepfather

Letter from a Stepfather

Dear Officer Babb,

    I have heard so much about your magical "Question Box" that I thought I should give it a try. My son (stepson I believe is the technical term) is one of your D.A.R.E. students. You seem to have achieved a "God-Like" status in David's life. Our family has come to look forward to dinner on D.A.R.E days. Your stories as well as the contents of your lessons, are the main topics for discussion. You seem to have a gift for working with young children. You have been able to penetrate the tough emotional armor, inside which my son seems to take refuge when he is around me.

    Now for my question! How is it, Officer Babb, that I can take a child at the age of seven, love him, clothe him, feed him, worship the ground that his mother walks on, truly accept him as my own son, and never once hear him refer to me as his "Dad"? Yet, you can spend less than an hour each week with him and manage to become his hero. I have tried for three years just to mean something in David's life, and have failed. I apologize for sounding somewhat bitter. I realize that I should be grateful that someone has been able to reach David, and I am. However, after trying so hard to be the person that he would eventually call "Dad," it is somewhat demoralizing to have someone else come along and instantly become his hero.

Please don't get me wrong. I do appreciate all that you and the other officers do. I wish you well in your efforts to save our nation's children.

Sincerely,
****

Note from the Author

It was this letter that postponed my resignation from the DARE program. The following is my response. The issues of parenting, divorce, and communicating with children will be addressed in greater detail throughout the final chapters of this text.

My Response

Dear Mr. ——— (we will refer to him as Mr. Samford),

The words do not exist to adequately express what receiving your letter has meant to me, both personally and professionally. I have been looking forward to meeting you at the DARE graduation. You see, Mr. Samford, you mean much more to David than you realize. I have learned so much about you that I feel as though I have known you for years. I know about the homemade kite that you and David built on his ninth birthday. You remember, the one that crashed into the neighbor's chimney. I know about the time you and David took turns sleeping on the kitchen floor, as you stood vigil over the family's sick pet. I also know about your recent heart attack. That was when David prayed several times each day, asking God to take his father rather than you.

You see, Mr. Samford, there is a tremendous difference between being a child's father and being a child's "Dad." Anyone can be a father, simply by conceiving a child. While the term "father" is an instantly achieved title, the title of "Dad" must be earned over a period of time. It is earned by helping your child build his first kite and by standing vigil over a child's sick and dying pet. It can only be achieved through years of loving, caring, crying, worrying, and being there. You know you have earned the title of "Dad" when your child prays several times a day for God to let you survive a heart attack. The term "Dad" is defined differently by each child. Keep loving your son, continue to be there for him, and you will become his definition of a "Dad."

David has been much more than just another one of my students. I have known for a long time that I have a special gift for working with children. However, it was David who first caused me to question that gift. You see, Mr. Samford, David has been a special challenge for me. He rarely participates in classroom discussions and has never volunteered to perform in classroom skits. I have tried my hardest to reach him, but had thought my efforts to have been in vain.

Having thought myself unsuccessful with David, I began to consider whether or not I was really making a difference in the lives of any of my students. Your letter attests to the fact that I have made a difference, in at least two lives. I have also come to realize that there are many more Davids in the world, whose lives have been touched by people like you and me, who are also wondering if their efforts have really made a difference.

The only classroom discussion in which David has actively participated was one in which students were asked to identify their heroes. David identified two of the heroes in his life. His first hero was his "Mom." His second hero was you. You see Mr. Samford, you **have** become David's "Dad," just as I now know that I **have** made a difference. We should consider ourselves fortunate. Just think of all the parents, teachers, counselors, and others who selflessly devote their lives to our children, who will never know for sure. Thank you for letting me know. Take care. I wish you well in your challenging role of "Daddyhood."

Sincerely,
Officer J. A. Babb

Note: For all of those who act as mentors to our children who may occasionally wonder if you have really made a difference. Think of "David" and realize that you have.

Chapter 8
Letters from Allison

Letter 1

Dear Officer ———,

How are you? I am OK. I guess. I'm sorry that I haven't written for so long but I lost your address and had to get it from Stacie's mother. Middle school is OK. I guess. I would like it a lot better if my friends were not changing so much. You remember the older boy that I told you Stacie was going out with, in the last letter I wrote to you? Well, I think he is going to get her in trouble. She really loves him a lot. They have even started having sex together. I told her that she was too young to start having sex. She says that when you have a boyfriend who is older you have to have sex because they are already used to getting it from the older girls. That's why I don't want an older boyfriend right now. Let them ruin someone else's life. Sorry! That probably sounded a little mean.

Here is the big problem, as if the other ones were little!!! Her boyfriend is in a gang called the WDs. Their girlfriends are in a gang called the WDQs. The "Q" stands for "Queens". The WDQs don't do much bad stuff. They just hang out together.

To get into the WDQs, she has to go through an initiation. She's not sure that she wants to do it, though. I'm really worried about her. I'm afraid that if I tell her mother what is going on, Stacie will stop talking to me. I think I may be the only *real* friend she has left. I guess that's it for the update. I promise not to take so long to write the next time.

Your friend,
Allison

P.S. Please write back soon.

Letter 2

Dear Officer ———,

Stacie has a major problem now!!! She finally told me what she is supposed to do for her gang initiation. To prove her loyalty to the gang, she has to be "trained" into the gang. That means that she has to have sex with all of the boys in the WDs, while they videotape her. Then if she ever tries to leave the gang, they will show the tape to other people. Stacie refused to go through with it and broke up with her boyfriend.

Last week the WDQs caught her as she was walking home from school. They beat her up real bad and then declared her a member of the gang (the WDQs). Her boyfriend came to her house the other night and they got back together.

Stacie's mother came to our house and asked if she could talk to me. I went ahead and told her everything. I told her that I no longer wanted to be Stacie's friend. Then she started crying and asked me to please keep being Stacie's friend. I told her that I would, but I don't really want to. Do you think that I should keep being Stacie's friend?

Your friend
Allison

P.S. I'll let you know what happens.

Letter 3

Dear Officer ———,

I knew I should have stopped being Stacie's friend. After I told her mother everything, she grounded Stacie and told her that she could not see her boyfriend anymore. Now Stacie is mad at me and I'm mad at her mom. I will never confide in her mom again. The other night some gang members came to our house and wrote "WDQs Rule" on our driveway. My dad called the police. Now my parents think that I'm in a gang with Stacie. I guess I should have taken your advice. Soorrry . . . I may listen to you the next time.

Your friend,
Allison

P.S. Are you mad at me for not listening to you?

P.S.S. Write back soon!!!

Letter 4

Dear Officer ———,

My mom told me that you talked to Stacie's mother before I told her about everything. My mom said that her mother didn't believe you until she talked to me. I guess Stacie should also be mad at you, but she's just mad at me. My mom said that I shouldn't be mad at you for telling, because you did the right thing. I was mad at you before, but I guess I kind of understand now. I'm still a little disappointed in you but I'll get over it some day. I guess you would do the same thing if it was me that was getting into trouble. My mom said that I should have told her earlier though.

Stacie is going to live with her father for a while. I

think that will probably help her. He's more strict than her mom. We haven't had anymore problems with the gang. Everything else is cool. I'll write you later.

Your friend,
Allison

From the Author

Maintaining a child's confidence can be a tough issue to deal with. It is only by virtue of having the child's confidence that we ever became privy to the previous information. However, I feel the child's safety and well-being should always be placed first, even at the risk of losing the child's confidence. Although I did not have access to the contributing officer's responses to Allison's letters, I do know that he contacted Stacie's mother following "Letter 2."

I chose to include this letter due to the fact that this and similar scenarios appear to be becoming more prevalent, especially with middle-school students. Although this particular scenario is a slightly more extreme scenario, gang initiations can include anything from having to commit a "minor" crime, such as theft, to having to commit a more serious crime, such as rape or murder. On occasion, some gangs will record these initiations on videotape. This may later be used as leverage to maintain the loyalties of a disgruntled gang member. As unpleasant as this issue may be, it needs to be addressed. The chapter entitled "Helpful Hints" will offer some suggestions for parents that may help to reduce the likelihood of their child ever becoming a victim of drugs, gangs, etc.

Chapter 9
Letters from Katie

Letter 1

Dear Officer Babb,

Since my daddy died a few years ago, my mom has been working at two jobs. She has one daytime job that she goes to every day during the week. She only goes to her nighttime job twice each week. She told me last night that she was going to start a part-time job on the weekends. She wants to make extra money so I can go to camp this summer. I told here that I did not like her having so many jobs because I don't get to see her much anymore. She said that she has to work extra jobs so we can keep living in a nice house and a good neighborhood and so we can still live like we did when my daddy was still living. I miss my daddy a lot because he died. I miss my mom too, even though she is still living. Sometimes I feel like I lost my mom too. Did you feel like this when your daddy died? Is there anything that I should do?

Sincerely,
Katie

Letter 2

Dear Officer Babb,

I decided to write the letter to my mom, like you

suggested. I put it on her bed so she would find it when she went to bed. I liked writing the letter because it gave me a long time to think about what I wanted to say and to make sure that I used the right words. In the letter, I told her how I felt. She brought ice cream to my room and woke me up, but I wasn't really asleep, though. We sat on my bed and talked for almost two hours.

I asked my mom what would happen to us if she only worked one job. She said that we would have to move to a smaller house or an apartment and that I would probably have to change schools. I told her that I would rather live in a smaller house if it meant that we could spend more time together. She said that we would have to think about what all of our options are. We hugged for a little while, but I was the only one that cried. My mom laid down with me until I made her think that I was asleep. Then she went back to her room.

When I went to the bathroom, I could hear my mom crying in her room. She never cries in front of me. I don't like it when she cries alone. I feel sadder when I cry alone. My grandmother said that it is okay for her to cry alone sometimes.

Sincerely,
Katie

P.S. Thanks for helping me. I think it was a good idea to write the letter.

From the Author: Regarding Katie

What a devoted mother!!! Katie's mother is primarily guilty of being a wonderful and loving mother, whose primary goal in life is to provide the very best life possible for her child. Unfortunately, however, there are often tradeoffs that have to be made. Providing the best of some things often comes at the cost of eliminating other, more essential things. Being aware of her daughter's concerns, Katie's mother has adjusted those tradeoffs.

F.Y.I.: Although Katie's mother continued working two jobs, she decided against taking the weekend job. Katie and her mom now have two special days of the week. One is "dessert night." One night each week they make a special dessert together. The other special day is their day. They set aside one day of the week for some special activity.

What A Parent!!!

Chapter 10
A Letter from David

David's Letter

Dear Officer Babb,
 Surprise, it's David from (*school*). I bet you never expected to get a letter from me. How is life treating you? I bet you're looking forward to the summer so you can have a break from teaching. Life has been hectic around here since my dad moved out. I guess I am kind of the man of the house now, not that anyone listens to me. I guess you are probably wondering why I am a writing, so I'll get to the point.
 The reason that I am writing now is to ask for advice on a problem that I have. Since Steve was cut up **[Steve received multiple stab wounds during a gang-related altercation]**, I have stopped hanging with the ——— **(name of David's former gang)**. Like you told us in fifth grade, "it's just not worth it." Since my dad left, my little brother is getting a major attitude and is starting to hang out with some gang members. I don't want him to make the same mistake that Steve and I made. When ever I try to warn him, he brings up my past gang involvement. It's hard to be a role model, when my past mistakes are continually thrown in my face.
 He always says, "You did the same thing. Why should

I listen to you?" I was hoping that you could give me some idea about how to become a role model to my little brother.

Thanks,
David

My Response

Dear David,

Yes, I was *pleasantly* surprised to hear from you. It sounds as though a lot has occurred in you life since your days as a fifth-grade "problem child." I was very sorry to hear about Steve. Hopefully others will learn from his tragedy. It sounds like you have. Now for the advice that you requested regarding your status as a role model.

There are two types of role models in this world. There are positive role models and there are negative role models. We can learn from both.

From *positive role models,* we learn how to achieve our goals and to realize our full potential.

From *negative role models,* we can learn how to avoid falling short of achieving those goals and of realizing our full potential.

As you can see, we can benefit from both types. Only you can make the decision as to which type of role model you wish to be. I would like to commend you on your responsible decision to become a positive role model.

Along with being a positive role model comes a tremendous amount of responsibility, the most crucial responsibility being that you do your best to make good decisions. However, when you do make a bad decision, which you will, that does not end your status as a positive role model. When you make a bad decision, you can continue being a positive role model by doing four things.

1. Take full responsibility for your decision.

2. Accept the consequences of the decision.
3. Learn any lessons offered by the decision.
4. Be willing to share that knowledge with those to whom you are a role model.

When your brother brings up the bad decisions of your past and asks why he should listen to you, try to explain it in the following manner. The reason he should listen to you is that you have made some bad decisions, as did Steve, and you have had to suffer the consequences of those decisions (share some of those consequences with him). You do not want your brother to make the same bad decisions. Steve was lucky because he got a second chance. Tell your brother that you are concerned that he may not get the second chance.

David, you have an opportunity to be a wonderful role model. You've "been there and done that." Share that knowledge with your brother and others in hope that they will not make the same bad decisions that you have made in the past. I guess I will go for now. Take care, good luck, and hang in there.

A role model,
Officer Babb

P.S. *You have made me proud.* Feel free to keep in touch.

Chapter 11
Letters from a Gangster's Girlfriend

Letter 1

Dear Officer ———,

I am sorry it took me so long to write back. I have a new boyfriend and we have been spending a lot of time together. He is in the eighth grade this year. He is the reason I decided to write you. Well, I would have written sooner or later anyway. This problem just made me write you sooner.

Like I told you earlier, I have a boyfriend in the eighth grade. I really like him a lot and we get along real well. Anyway, the problem is that he is in a gang. They are a real bad gang. He said that when him and his friend joined the gang that they didn't really do bad stuff. As more people joined the gang, they started doing bad stuff like hurting people and stealing things. I told him that I wished he would get out of the gang. He said that he does not want to be in the gang, but he can not get out. When I asked him why he could not get out, he said that he could not talk about it. I am worried that he will get into trouble if he stays in the gang. I better go now. Please write back soon.

Friends forever,
****

Letter 2

Dear Officer ———,

    I hope you are ready for a new problem, because I have a big one. You remember that my boyfriend is in a gang, but does not want to be. He finally told me why he could not get out of the gang. When he got into the gang, he had to go through a gang initiation. He broke into a car and stole some stuff while the gang members videotaped it. He said that if he tries to leave the gang, they will give the videotape to the police. He is afraid of getting in trouble with the police. He has never been in any big trouble before.

    I like him a lot, but I do not think I should keep going out with him if he stays in the gang. What do you think we can do? Can you please write soon and give me some advice?

Friends forever,
****

Officer's Response

Dear ———,

    Thank you for staying in touch. I was about to answer your earlier letter when I received this one. It sounds like you and your boyfriend have some decisions to make. No advice that I could offer would be a foolproof solution. Regardless of what the ultimate solution is, it will not be easy. However, as I told you once before, the right thing to do is not always the easiest thing to do.

    The best advice that I can offer your boyfriend is to consider the following steps.

        1. Consider the worst possible consequences of remaining in the gang.

2. Consider the worst possible consequences of the tape being turned over to the police.
3. Steps #1 and #2 are his options. Choose the option that has the least severe negative consequences.

    Assuming that he will choose option #2, he should consider the following.
4. Take full responsibility for his actions, including the burglary of the vehicle.
5. Be prepared to accept the consequences of his actions.
6. Once he does this, he has eliminated the gang's bargaining tool. The gang should be left with nothing to hold over your boyfriend.
7. If he truly wishes to no longer be a part of the gang, then he should be able to get out.

That is best advice that I can offer your boyfriend. Now for you! You have several decisions to make, that only you can make. Obviously those decisions will depend, in part, on the decisions that your boyfriend makes. My best advice to you is to follow your head, rather than your heart, on this one. I feel confident that you will make the right decisions. I guess I will go for now. Take care and please stay in touch.

Friends,
Officer ****

P.S. Have you talked to either of your parents about this?

From the Author

The gang issue will be addressed in greater detail, in chapter 19, **"Even More Letters from 'Anonymous.'"**

In addition, the chapter will discuss measures that may be taken to reduce the likelihood that your child will ever become a victim of gang violence.

Chapter 12
More Letters from "Anonymous"

Anonymous Student

Dear Officer ———,

My dad does not believe in hitting children, even when they are bad. When we are bad, he yells at us, instead of spanking us. But when we do something that really makes him mad, he yells and says really mean things that hurt my feelings. Sometimes when I make a mistake, he asks me if I am stupid or something. When I tell him that I am not stupid, he tells me that I act like I am. Sometimes I think it would be better for him to spank us, because the pain goes away a lot quicker than when he says bad things that hurt my feelings. I know my dad loves us and does not mean all of the mean things that he says to us.

Sincerely,
One of your students

P.S. I have tried talking to him about it, but he does not think that he says that many bad things to us.

P.S.S What should I do?

Anonymous Student

Dear Officer ———,
 I am the one who has the dad that doesn't believe in hitting children. I wrote you the letter about the bad things that my dad says to me sometimes. I did what you said in class. Every time I heard my dad say something bad to me or my brother, I wrote it down in my notebook. I wrote the date, time, and what he said.
 After a week, I tried to give it to him, but he wouldn't take it. After he went to bed, I taped it to the bathroom mirror so he would see it in the morning when he was getting ready for work. It didn't work, though. My mom found the note before she went to bed and took it to my dad.
 They got into a big fight (they didn't hit each other or anything, they just yelled). I heard my mom ask him if he was stupid. I guess he must know what it feels like now. Maybe he will stop saying bad things to us now. Sorry that your plan didn't work. Thanks for trying to help me, though.

Sincerely,
One of your students

Anonymous Student

Dear Officer Babb,
 You remember when you asked how many of us play sports or have other interests and then you asked how many of us like football? When I raised my hand for liking football, I sorta lied. I do play football, but I don't really like it much. I do it to make my dad proud. I like when he comes to the games to watch me. Except when I don't play very well. Whenever we lose, my dad spends the next few days telling me what I did wrong. Then he always says, "I'm going to make a football player out of you yet." My dad

was a big football star in high school and college. I am glad he wants me to be like him, but I also want to be myself. I liked playing baseball, but my dad hardly ever came to the games. Sometimes I think I should get into something really bad like gangs or drugs or something. Then me liking baseball wouldn't be that big of a deal, compared to gangs or drugs. Don't worry, I won't get into drugs. I know my dad loves me. Sometimes I think he just misses being a kid. I wonder if his dad did the same thing to him.

Sincerely,
?????

PS. I wish we had one of these question boxes in my house.

From the Author

This last letter gives a not uncommon scenario. Much like that of a friend of mine, whose father owns a funeral service. He has worked very hard over the years to build this business that he intends on passing to his son. However, the son hasn't the slightest interest in pursuing the family business. In our scenario, the father is obviously proud of his son. The son is willing to make virtually any sacrifice to keep his dad's approval and to make him proud, even if it means being miserable. Now we have a case in which a child is miserable, but doesn't know how to tell his dad, and a proud father, who may be trying to relive his younger days vicariously through his son, who hasn't a clue as to how miserable his son is. Each thinks the other is happy. Each is very fortunate to have the other. The son is fortunate to have a father who is so interested and involved in his child's life. The father is fortunate to have a son who is so interested in pleasing his dad and earning his approval.

So what is the solution to this dilemma? **Communication!!!** The son needs to talk and the dad needs to listen. Due to the anonymous nature of this letter, my options for responding were limited. Following a class discussion, with a revised scenario, the students agreed with me that a letter would be a possible means of initiating a dialogue between the child and his father.

Anonymous Student

Dear Officer ———,

Mrs. ——— said that I should apologize for being late to school and missing part of your class. But I was already sorry before she told me to be. I just was not going to say anything. Anyway!!! I am sorry that I was late for your class. When I get up in the mornings, I have to get me and my brothers ready for school and then fix them breakfast. This morning when I walked my brothers to the bus stop, I remembered that I forgot to wake up my mom, so she could get ready for work. I was late because I had to go back home to get her up. Then she wanted me to make her pop tarts. I won't be late tomorrow, though. Whenever I'm late for school, my mom says I have to wake up thirty minutes earlier on the next day, so I won't be late again.

Your best student,
You know who!

From the Author

Although this is a rather extreme example, this scenario is not at all uncommon within single-parent families. This child has become a casualty of "parentization." The process of parentization is discussed in greater detail in **chapter 26, "Divorce: From a Child's Perspective."**

Anonymous Student

Dear Officer ———,
When you were little, did you ever feel like your parents were making you grow up too fast? I try to be serious when I am around my parents and their friends. I do all of the activities that they want me to, so they will be proud of me. Sometimes, when I want to do regular kid things, I can tell that they get disappointed. I don't mind growing up, but I want to enjoy being a kid first. Instead of peer pressure, I have parent pressure.

You are so cooool,
Me

From the Author

The sentiments expressed in this letter are indicative of those that are expressed by my students who live in the more affluent school communities.

The manner in which I responded to this particular issue with the students should not be as important as the message this letter should send to parents. It is only natural for parents to want the very best for their children and to encourage them to realize their full potential in life. While this pressure is a healthy and necessary aspect of parenting, we must remain cognizant of how this pressure is being processed by our children. The best way to achieve this level of cognizance is to communicate with your child, his peers, educators, and mentors.

I generally respond to this issue by having the students consider why these pressures and demands are placed upon them. I also share with them examples of the other extreme, having parents who couldn't care less. I always conclude the discussion with an appeal for the students to share their feelings and concerns with their parents. I have seen too many tragedies involving children occur that could have been prevented by communication between parents and their children.

Anonymous Student

Dear Officer ———,
Why do parents not like to argue in front of girls? My parents argue in front of me and my brother sometimes, but if my sister comes into the room, they stop arguing and say that they will talk about it later. I think it's because they don't want to upset her. I guess they think that I will not get upset because I'm a boy, but I do. I don't think they should argue in front of boys either.

Signed,
A Boy

From the Author

Keep this letter in mind when you read the chapter entitled "An Afterthought," near the end of this book.

Anonymous Student

Dear Officer Babb,
    How can I just be myself and keep all of my friends? When I'm around certain friends, I have to act a certain way so they will still like me. Then when I am around other friends, I have to act a different way so they will like me. I want to have friends, but I also want to be myself. I wish people would just let me be the way I am. What can I do?
    Not Signed

My Response to the Class

After reading the letter aloud to the class, I shared the following story with the students.

When I was in the fifth grade, my teacher had a small piece of wood on her desk. On this piece of wood was carved a short proverb. Although I did not fully understand its significance, at the time, this proverb has stayed in my memory for all of these years. Although I do not recall the author's name, if there was one listed, the proverb went as follows:

> He who carves himself to suit others,
> will soon whittle himself away.

(I then asked the students to tell me what the proverb meant to them. Following a brief discussion, I summed up the responses as follows.)

Each one of you is special in some way. Each of you has something unique to offer the world, that no one else can offer. That is *yourself.* Your values and beliefs, your special skills and talents, your personality and sense of humor are what help to create that uniqueness. If you continually change yourself to appease others, you will gradually deplete that uniqueness, thereby, depriving the world of what you have to offer. No matter how you act, you will never be able to please everyone.

Therefore, it makes more sense to always be yourself and to allow others to be themselves. Do your best to treat others with respect and kindness. If they still do not like you, whose problem is it? It is their own loss.

Anonymous Student

Dear Officer Babb,

My brother is in seventh grade and says that there are a lot of gangs in middle school. He said that sometimes they pick on people for no reason. One of my brother's friends got beaten up by a gang because of the kind of clothes he was wearing. How will I know what kind of clothes not to wear? Also, how do I keep the gangs from messing with me.

Note

A primary concern and fascination of my students is the issue of gangs. With middle school in their near future, many students are concerned with how to avoid wearing clothing that may cause them to be targeted by a gang and how to identify gang members, so they can avoid contact with them.

Response to the Class

I am not as concerned with your becoming involved

with gangs as I am that you may become a victim of gang violence. It has been my experience that a majority of those who become victims of gang violence are not in any way associated with the gang. They are usually innocent bystanders. In some cases the victim happens to be a sleeping child whose bed just happened to be located near a bedroom window or a student who happened to be wearing the "wrong" type of tennis shoes or sports jacket.

Although there is no way to guarantee that you will never become a victim, there are a few precautions that you can take to lessen the chances that you will ever become a victim of gang violence. They are:

1. Do not hang out with known gang members.
2. Do not hang out near known gang hangouts.
3. Do not wear known gang clothing.
4. Do not display gang hand signs.
5. Do not draw gang graffiti (not even on your notebook).
6. Do not openly criticize or challenge gang members.
7. Do not take valuables or large amounts of money to school.
8. Take the gang threat seriously and realize that no one is immune.
9. When possible, try to do things with a friend or a group of friends.

As for being able to identify students who are associated with a gang, do not worry. You will know which students are in a gang, what type of clothing they wear, and where they hang out. I guarantee that you will know. My former students have verified this fact. I do not want you to be intimidated by the thought of going to middle school. Thousands of students have a very successful and rewarding experience in middle school. There is no reason why your experience should be any different. Just take common-sense precautions and use good judgment; make responsible decisions.

Chapter 13
Letters from Stephanie

Letter 1

Dear Officer Babb,

    I am sorry that I have taken so long to write you. My mom said to thank you for the nice card. My parents liked it a lot. You told me to let you know how I am doing. Well, I am not doing very well. I feel so lonely with my dad gone. He is going to a business school in California for four months. I miss him so much. I wish he did not have to be away for so long. This is the longest that he has ever been away from me. He calls us every night, but I only get to talk to him for a few minutes. It is not the same as having him here. He usually sits by my bed at night and tells me about his day, while I fall asleep. I can still smell him when I walk by my parents' bedroom. My dad wears the same kind of cologne that you do. He will be away for two more months. What do you do when you miss someone so much? I guess I will go for now. Thanks for listening and please write back soon.

Love,
Stephanie

From the Author

Stephanie is a precious ten-year-old girl who is very close

to her father. Each day, during school lunch, she had been calling him at work to ask how his day is going. The following is my reply to her letter.

My Response

Dear Stephanie,

Thank you very much for the letter. I am sorry to hear of your loneliness. However, not to worry, I am an expert at this loneliness stuff. Each person copes with loneliness in a different way. Each situation requires the use of different coping skills. The following ideas may or may not work for you. However, here are three suggestions that may help.

First, ask your mother for one of your father's work shirts. Have her **lightly** spray it with your father's cologne. Then put his shirt around one of the pillows that you sleep with at night.

Second, ask if it would be OK to record a nightly phone conversation with your dad. Once you have recorded it, do not listen to it until you are ready to go to bed. Then set the tape recorder near your bed and listen to it as you fall asleep.

Although you and your dad are many miles apart, the distance is not really as great as it may seem. When each of you looks into the sky at night, you both see the same moon and the same stars. My **third** suggestion is for you to locate a constellation, such as the Big Dipper (Ursa Major). Select one star to represent you at home and another star to represent your father at his distant location. Arrange a time in the evening when you and your father can both look into the sky. While concentrating on each other's star, you can say "good night" to one another. For a brief moment, the distance between you will not seem as great.

I realize that none of these suggestions can take the place of having your dad home again. However, I hope they can help make the loneliness a little more bearable until your dad returns. Your parents are very fortunate to have such a wonderful daughter. Take care and stay safe.

Your buddy,
Officer Babb

Letter 2

Dear Officer Babb,

Thank you for writing back so soon. My dad is coming home in four weeks. I can't wait! My parents appreciated the suggestions that you gave to us. We also picked a special star for my mom. She misses dad almost as much as I do. We want you to come over for dinner sometime. My mom also wants you to meet my aunt. You will probably meet her when you come for dinner. I think you will like her. She is smart and very pretty. I guess I will go for now. Please write back soon.

Love,
Stephanie

Chapter 14
Letters from Diana

Letter 1

Dear Officer ———,
 Hi,
 Sorry I have not been writing you, but I am so busy with school. Junior high is cool and fun, but a lot of my friends are changing. Leeza has changed so much. She is hanging around a girl that has parties with older guys that bring beer and marijuana. She **(the girl)** smokes and keeps trying to get Leeza to also. I don't even talk to her. I have just been trying to warn Leeza about her.
 Leeza shaved the back of her head and wears weird clothes now. Her mother won't let her wear them, so she leaves her house with normal clothes and changes in to the weird ones at school. It's like she has a whole other life now, from her normal one and her family doesn't know. She also sneaks out sometimes at night, to hang out with this older guy. He is in a gang called the HDs.

Your Pen Pal,
Diana

 P.S. Junior high is not as good without an officer around to help with problems. I mean I can still talk to you, but now I have to send you a letter, which takes a lot longer for you give me advice or help me think of what to do.

Letter 2

Dear Officer Babb,
    Hi,
    I have a really big problem and my mother said it was OK for you to call our house so I can talk to you about it. I will tell you a little now, so you can be thinking about it.
    You remember that I told you about Leeza sneaking out of her house to be with that older guy. Well, she lost her virginity to him. She's just turned 12!!! She is really falling for this guy, big time! Last weekend, she told her mother that she was spending the weekend with a friend (that girl that I told you about, in my last letter). She spent Friday night with her boyfriend and Saturday night with her friend. Please call me. My parents said it's OK.

                                    Your Pen Pal,
                                      Diana

P.S. Our phone number is ***-****

From the Author: Regarding Diana

Diana comes from a very affluent family. She has two brothers, to whom she is very close. She has two wonderful parents who are very involved in her life.

    Diana is having a difficult time, dealing with the changes that are occurring in some of her friends, as they make the transition, from elementary school to a middle-school environment. Fortunately, she has a very healthy support system. Diana enjoys listening to music, especially the "Cranberries." She also enjoys roller skating, and is just starting to think that boys are OK. She hopes to be a cheerleader next year.

    Although I responded to Diana's dilemma in person

and via telephone, I will share some of the more important aspects of our discussion. I began by referring to one of our previous lessons in which we addressed the possible changes that will take place, not only with their peers but within themselves as well.

I explained to the students that as they progress in life, their values, goals, and interests will be shaped by personal experiences. People tend to socialize with others who have values and interests that are similar to their own. Friends who share common interests and spend much of their time together in elementary school may grow apart during their middle-school years. While this does not signal the demise of the friendship, it does change the dynamics of that relationship. These changes will lead some of their friends in a positive direction while having the opposite effect on others. During this process of growth, each person will have some very important decisions to make regarding which path they want to take, the negative or the positive.

In Diana's case, she fulfilled her responsibility as a friend, by sharing her concerns with Leeza. The responsibility now lies with Leeza, as she has some important decisions to make regarding the path she will choose in her life. As I told Diana, there is nothing wrong with trying to be there for Leeza. However, there needs to be a limit. That limit should fall short of allowing herself to be drawn down the same negative path. In short, no one can be there for Leeza until Leeza is there for herself.

Update:

Being there for Leeza was beginning to take a toll on Diana. As Leeza's life took a serious turn for the worse, she attempted to take Diana down with her. Leeza wanted Diana to steal from her home to help Leeza purchase drugs for her boyfriend. She told Diana that if she was a true friend she would help her. Diana responded by saying, "If you are a true friend you would not ask me to do this." Diana has finally let go.

Chapter 15
Letters from a "White Girl"

A Note from the Author

In this particular case, I feel it is important to introduce you to the student prior to reading the letters. Throughout this chapter, you will occasionally encounter ethnic references. This is unfortunately due to the fact that ethnicity has been made an issue in this particular situation. The following letters are from one of my middle-school students named Rachael. Rachael is one of the most wonderful human beings that you could ever meet. She is intelligent, witty, friendly, very outgoing, and just loves being with people. Few people cross Rachael's path without becoming one of her many friends. As I accompany her through the halls, en route to her next class, Rachael is greeted by virtually every student who passes her, especially the boys. I guess I failed to mention that she is quite attractive also. Rachael is Hispanic and attends a large (1,800 + students), ethnically diverse middle school. As you may have guessed, she is a fairly popular student. Armed with this information, we may now proceed to her letters.

Letter 1

Dear Officer Babb,

I have a small problem that seems to be getting bigger as each day passes. The other day I was sitting with my friends during lunch. This girl who was sitting a few tables away kept staring me down. I didn't know who she was, so I couldn't figure out why she would be staring me down. Just before lunch ended, she came over to our table and just stood behind me. I turned and asked if anything was wrong. She said that she wanted to fight me. When I asked her why she wanted to fight me, she just walked away. She went back and sat with her "clique." I can't imagine why she wants to fight me. I've never done anything to her. All I know about her is that she is new in school and always hangs out with a clique of Hispanic girls. They're not really a gang. They just only hang out with each other.

Later in the day she also told a few of my friends that she was going to fight me. So I went up to her and asked again why she wanted to fight me.

She still did not answer me. If I am going to fight her, I would at least like to know why. I will let you know what happens. See you at school.

Your Good Friend,
Rachael

Letter 2

Dear Officer Babb,

Aren't you lucky! Two letters from me in two days. Well, I finally found out why that girl wants to fight me. She said that I act too much like a white girl so I can fit in with my white friends. I was so freaked by what she said that I didn't know how to respond to her. So I just walked away. I act like the person that I am. My personality doesn't come from being Hispanic. It comes from the way I was raised and the things that I have experienced in my life. I almost want to ask her what I do that makes her think that I am acting like a "white person." Then maybe I could at least understand why she is so upset. I am happy just the way I am and don't plan on changing. If she wants to fight me, I guess I will just have to fight her. I'll go for now. See ya the next time you come for a visit. Try to come during lunch.

Your Good Friend,
Rachael

My Response

Dear Rachael,

Two letters within the same week! I feel honored! After reading your last letter, I am tempted to ask the same question of your peer. Exactly which behaviors constitute "acting White?" Let's see now. You are mature, friendly, kind, considerate, outgoing, intelligent, witty, and respectful of others. If she feels, that possessing or displaying these traits constitutes "acting White," then it is a good indicator of how she views not only herself but her culture as well. The fact of this matter is that you *are* Hispanic and you *do* possess these wonderful human qualities. Therefore, you are acting as much Hispanic as you are "acting White" or any other ethnicity. Consider a world in which every member of each culture believes as you do. Now compare that to a world in which every member of each culture feels as this other girl feels. In which world would you prefer to live? As you already know and this girl has yet to learn, respecting your own culture and honoring your heritage does not have to come at the expense of disrespecting the culture and heritage of others.

I will offer one final point. It is due to the very traits

and qualities for which this girl is criticizing you, that you will be very successful in life. It is only by overcoming her own ignorance and ethnocentric attitude that this girl will ever become a successful and productive member of society. You are a good girl and a wonderful human being. Continue to think for yourself and do not allow others to dictate your values, your ethics, or your life. I guess I will go for now. Take care and good luck.

Your friend,
Officer Babb

P.S. Thanks for staying in touch.

From the Author

Some may wonder why I have chosen to include this particular chapter. It has been my observation that scenarios similar to the one involving Rachael are not only common but are occurring with increasing frequency. In spite of valiant efforts on the part of schools, churches, and other community institutions to encourage assimilation, tolerance, and acceptance, there is a growing pressure within some cultures/subcultures for separation or segregation, especially among our youth. While the preceding observations will no doubt cause me to acquire a variety of labels from critics, the fact remains that "Facts are facts." Until we, as a culturally diverse society, can foster an environment and create a forum in which people will have the courage to acknowledge and openly discuss the true facts, we may never solve the problem.

From my own observations, this pressure to conform appears to be less prevalent in the more affluent schools and is *virtually* nonexistent in private schools (at least the private schools that I have visited). On a positive and seemingly contradictory note, I have also observed a greater effort on the part of my students to understand, appreciate, and respect other cultures and subcultures. In my discussions with other educators regarding these issues, it has been suggested that the latter may be the impetus behind the increasing pressure to "culturally conform." Some have even suggested that, when considering the larger picture, this may actually be a positive sign. The fact that "acting White, Black, Hispanic, etc.," or "crossing over," as some of my students put it, has become a bigger issue indicates that many more of today's youth view themselves and their societal roles in the context of a larger multicultural society rather than in the more limited context of a small unicultural society. Hopefully this also indicates that many of today's youth realize that the greatness and uniqueness of our nation lies in its cultural diversity.

Chapter 16
Letters from Maggie and Her Mother

Letter 1

Dear Officer Babb,
    I found out this weekend that my parents are getting a divorce. I found out first from my brother. So I went and asked my dad if it was true. He said "yes," but it wasn't a good time to talk about it. So I went and asked my mom why they were getting a divorce. She said it was because they fight a lot. She said that she still loves my dad, but they can no longer live together.
    I love my brother, but we fight a lot. Can they make us get a divorce too? Because I don't want to live a way from my brother.

Your worried friend,
Maggie

    P.S. Will you please please please answer this letter soon.

From the Author

At the age of nine, Maggie is the younger of two children.

Letter 2

Dear Officer Babb,

I finally made my dad talk to me. Sometimes, when I make him think that I am upset with him, I can make him do things. Sometimes, if it costs him money, it doesn't work though.

I asked my dad if he still loves my mom. He said that he loves her, but that he is no longer in love with her. He also said that when people fall out of love, it is hard for them to live together in the same house.

Do you think that he could ever fall out of love with me. I mean, I know that he is supposed to love me because I'm his daughter, but what happens if he falls out of love with me or my brother. I think that when you tell someone that you love them, you should mean it forever.

Your friend,
Maggie

P.S. Have you ever just stopped loving someone that you used to love?

Letter 3

Dear Officer Babb,

I wrote the letter to my mom and dad like you said to and made an appointment to talk to them together. They sat down together in our study like they were in trouble. I told them what I have been telling you.

Now I get to go see a mind doctor. Maybe he can tell me how to fix their minds.

Your friend,
Maggie

P.S. My mom is writing you a letter. If you get in

trouble, don't worry. She doesn't stay mad long, only at my dad.

   P.S.S. Thanks again for being my friend.

Letter from Maggie's Mother

Dear Officer Babb,
   I am Maggie's mother. She has told us a lot about you. I understand that she has told you a lot about us (the problems that my husband and I are currently having). While I am not thrilled with the personal nature of the information she shared with you, I do appreciate that you took the time to listen to her. More importantly, my husband and I appreciate the fact that you encouraged Maggie to speak to us about her concerns.
   I guess my husband and I were so involved with our own situation that we did not realize the effect our problems were having on the children.
   Maggie seems to have a great deal of trust in you. I hope that we can also trust in your discretion. Thank you again for what you do.

                                              Sincerely,
                                              ****

Letter to Maggie's Parents

Dear Mr. & Mrs. ———,
   Thank you very much for the nice letter and the kind words. As I am certain you have heard many times before, you have a wonderful daughter. Maggie is not only intelligent, witty, and outgoing; but she is a good person as well. She has been a joy to teach.
   It has been refreshing to see the tremendous amount

of love and respect that Maggie has for you and for her brother. I know that she will appreciate the tremendous amount of love and respect that she will receive from you as she attempts to understand and to cope with challenges that lie ahead for your family.

Please do not be concerned about the information that Maggie has shared. Her trust is well placed with me. I was concerned much less with what Maggie shared with me than I was with why she chose to share it with me. It is more important that she ultimately shared it with you. I wish your family good luck with the difficult challenges that lie ahead.

Sincerely,
Officer Babb

Chapter 17
Letters from Stephan and Tamara

Stephan

Dear Officer Babb,

    I told my mother what you told us about faith. That sometimes having faith means believing when it doesn't make sense to do so. I also told her that you said we should have faith in our parents, that the stuff they do is usually in our best interest. I think she likes you now. Probably because you were on her side. I told her that you were not married.

Your student,
Stephan

P.S. By the way, my mom isn't married either.

Tamara

Officer Babb,

    Thank you for DARE Bear. I liked getting to hold him for so long. People don't hang around me usually. When I had DARE Bear, I was real popular and everyone wanted to be around me. I felt like I had a lot of friends. But when I gave the bear back to you, people stopped hanging around me. I am not upset or anything. I just wanted to tell you thanks.

Your student,
Tamara

P.S. I will hold DARE bear again, if you need me to.

P.S.S. Can you tell how I can make more friends?

From the Author

DARE Bear is, in a sense, our classroom mascot. He is a small teddy bear that loves to be held and can never be left alone. It is a tremendous honor to hold DARE Bear. During each lesson, one student is chosen to hold DARE Bear.

Self-esteem is a tremendous issue with children. I often receive letters similar to Tamara's in which students are concerned that they do not fit in with their peers, or that they are always the last to be chosen when teams are picked, or that they never get invited to parties. While volumes could be written regarding self-esteem, I chose to include this letter as a reminder to parents that the self-esteem is an issue of great prominence in the lives of our children. It is important for parents to be aware of their child's social development. Observe their social skills when they are interacting with their peers. Many times, as in Tamara's case, poor social skills may be the cause of a child being ostracized by his or her peers.

In Tamara's case, we role-played various scenarios, which enabled us to polish her social skills a bit. In addition to the role playing, I offered Tamara the same advice that was offered in a previous anonymous letter.

Try your very best at everything that you do and treat others with respect. If they still do not like you, then it becomes their own problem and is their own loss. In closing I advised Tamara that the best way to make a friend is to be a friend. I can not express enough the importance of the self-esteem issue. It can literally distinguish the difference between the life and death or the success and failure of your child.

Chapter 18
Letters from Brittaney

Letter 1

Dear Officer ———,

Last Wed. I was at home and I was doing a school project that had to do with using glue and glitter. I had everything spread out on the living room when someone rang the doorbell. It was my friend, so I opened the door and let her in. My dog is really hyper when someone comes over, so he jumped all over her. When my friend sat down by my project, my dog followed her and stepped on the wet glue. He completely ruined my project. I started saying cause words (**curse words**) and I kicked him. Then he ran from me and tracked glitter and glue on the carpet. He tried to hide under the table but I yanked him out by his ear and slapped him on his nose. Then he used the bathroom on the floor and I got really mad. I dragged him into my sister's closet and didn't let him out. He was crying for a while. Ten minutes later I let him out and was being nice to him and kissing him. I feel bad too. I don't know if that's normal. I only get like that when I am mad. He made me so mad I couldn't help it.

Sincerely,
Brittaney

P.S. You are my best buddy. Even if you don't always agree with me.

From the Author

The behavior described in Brittaney's letter is obviously symptomatic of a greater problem. After reading her remaining letters, you will have a better understanding of source from which her rage comes.

Letter 2

We're still living with Bobby. I hate him so much. He's so mean. My mom has hardly no money, and Bobby has all the money he needs. He buys all this stuff for himself and never buys anything for us, not even my mom. I know this is never going to end. It'll keep going till we are begging on the streets. My mom tries so hard to please him, that she forgets about us. It's like we don't even exist.

I really don't like being in counseling. I hate to talk about this stuff to teachers, except for Mrs. ———, she's all right to talk to. I mean you are a police officer and you're real good at understanding kids, so you know what it's like. I can just talk to you better. But I'll keep on doing it (counseling) since you think I need to. I don't want to be your favorite student, but you are a good friend. It's cool to have a grown up friend to talk to. Just thought you would like to know.

Oh! There's one more thing. At school I don't feel like I'm good enough for my friends. I always seem to do something wrong when I'm around them. It seems like I am always saying I'm sorry to them and kissing their feet. I wanted to let you know this early, so you can have time to think about it before the next time we talk. That way you will already know what to tell me. I really have to go now.

Sincerely,
Brittaney

P.S. Are you tired of listening to my problems yet? I hope not, because it helps me a lot having someone to talk to that understands.

Letter 3

Dear Officer ———,
I have to write the day and what happened this week, from Wed. night to this Wed. morning. Some things I might talk to you about so read carefully.

Wed. night: Bobby left, won't be back till Sun.

Thurs.: Bobby is still gone.

Friday: My mom and I went out to eat. It was the first time we have done something fun together in a long time. Usually when Bobby is gone, she goes out looking for a new boyfriend.

Sat.: My mom really screams at my brother and tells him that she will never take him anywhere again. Bobby is still gone.

Sun.: My mom goes to the mall like she always does to hang around some guy she is seeing. But she doesn't really go to the mall. She just tells us that. Now she pays no attention to me. I love her very much. It hurts me when I can't spend time with her.
My mom must think I'm stupid. I know what she is doing and I know it's wrong. Since I have to keep it a secret from Bobby, it makes me feel like I'm doing something wrong along with her. What really hurts is that she doesn't

even ask me to keep it a secret. She automatically thinks that I will, which means she must think I'm like her.

Mon.: My mom got real mad at me. I told her that she never comes to anything at school or to watch me dance. I never ask my dad to come. I never really had someone close to me in distance and in my heart. My mom is so close in my heart, but she seems so far away. I feel like I am her friend, but sometimes I don't feel like she is my friend. It always makes me want to cry when I talk about my mom and about her never spending time with me. Oh! Bobby is home. I thought he was suppose to come back Sun. Anyway, they didn't talk to each other. I really want to talk to you about this.

Tues and Wed: Nothing happened. Bye!

Sincerely,
Brittaney

Letter 4

Dear Officer ———,
My mom and Bobby are getting a divorce. She is starting to get serious with the guy at the mall. I hope this one doesn't hate kids. She always goes out with much older men. Most of them have already raised their own children. They don't want to go through raising kids again, especially if they are someone else's kids. I hope this one doesn't mind having kids around. The only thing I don't like about her dating people is that we don't see her as much, because she is always with the guy. If this guy likes kids, maybe they will let us go with them sometimes. Thanks for listening.

Sincerely,
Brittaney

From the Author: Regarding Brittaney

Brittaney comes from an upper-middle-class home where she lives with her mother, her older sister, and her younger brother. She is a beautiful, mature, and extremely intelligent girl who is wise well beyond her young years. Unfortunately, her wisdom comes from all that she has had to endure in her young life. She loves gymnastics, reading, and writing poetry.

Brittaney is very selective about her friends, as well as in whom she confides. She loves her mother very much and longs for that special mother-daughter relationship. Unfortunately, I cannot reveal much about her father, other than to say that he is rarely in the picture.

I chose to include these letters from Brittaney because of what they reveal about how our children perceive, and are affected by, our actions. In reading the several hundred letters that I have received from children, I have been amazed at how closely our actions are watched and scrutinized by our children. After all, we are their role models. We are expected to be their primary source, from which they develop the life skills necessary to become responsible, productive members of society. The younger children watch what we do and just accept our actions and decisions as proper. As they grow and experience life, our children begin to accept less and to question more. This is a natural and healthy progression toward establishing their own independent identity and system of values.

This is also when the level of respect that our children have for their parents is either diminished or enhanced. If it is enhanced, we will continue to be their primary source for acquiring advice and life skills. If their respect for us is diminished, they will begin to seek out other sources for acquiring those same necessities. Brittaney's letters should serve as a reminder that our children are watching us. The old adage "Do as I say not as I do" no longer works and will cause you to lose their respect "in a heartbeat." When parents do make a mistake, as any parent is certain to do at some point, we are afforded a golden opportunity. Children realize we are not perfect. Therefore, their respect for us is enhanced when we can admit to this fact.

Chapter 19
Even More Letters from "Anonymous"

Anonymous Student

Dear Officer Babb,
 I have a problem that I want to tell you about. The other night 2 of my friends spent the night at my house. We let three other boys sneak in through my bedroom window and turned my radio on, so my parents couldn't hear anything. We started playing that game called spin the bottle, but we played with a can instead of a bottle. We just kissed on the lips at first, but later we French-kissed. When we stopped playing for a little while, my best friend feel asleep, but her boyfriend stayed awake. When we started playing spin the bottle again, my best friend's boyfriend spinned the can first. When it pointed at me, we French-kissed again. Later on, me and her boyfriend climbed out the window and walked to the park. We stayed at the park for a long time, but all we did was kiss and talked. We fell asleep and didn't wake up until it started getting day time. He walked me back to my bedroom window and then he left. I didn't get caught, but I have another problem anyway. I really like this boy a lot and he wants to start going out **("going out" replaced the old phrases "going together" and "going steady")**. I also love my best friend and don't want her to stop being my friend. So what do you think I should do.

From the Author

For obvious reasons, I chose not to read this letter aloud to the class. However, realizing that this was a real life scenario that the children could relate to, I took full advantage of the "teachable moment" that it presented. I learned early on, in my teaching experience, to take full advantage of every "teachable moment" that presents itself. Although I chose not to read this particular letter aloud to the class, I did create a similar and more appropriate scenario, one which was more parent proof and career safe.

After presenting the modified scenario, I had the students consider the possible consequences of the situation. Although I directed the discussion, the students supplied the topics. I was very impressed with the issues they addressed, some of which I had not even considered. The students covered such issues as personal safety, earning and maintaining parental trust, protecting one's own reputation, and loyalty to friends. It has been my experience that the best advice for children sometimes comes from within themselves. I could not have offered better wisdom and advice than that which came from these students. The letter had been word processed, and was not signed.

My primary purpose for including this particular letter was not to "snitch off" the children to their parents regarding their covert activities. This is really not an unusual scenario for elementary and middle-school kids today. Rather, I chose to include this particular letter in order to reinforce a previously made point. As far as their parents knew, these children were safely tucked in bed. Little did they know that just beyond their daughter's bedroom door, the girls were hosting a coed "make-out party," which culminated with a romantic stroll to the park, and their daughter spending the night under the stars with her best friend's boyfriend. Realizing that kids are going to be kids, it is important to realize that, as parents, we can not always be present to guide our children. Accepting this reality as a fact of life, it is important that we prepare our children as early as possible to deal responsibly with the infinite variety of pressures that they may encounter on their own.

P.S. You do not have to use much imagination to realize the possible decisions this girl would be having to deal with if this scenario were to have occurred in a high-school environment.

Anonymous Student

To Officer ———,
Me and my friend went to the store on Saturday to play video games and get some stuff for my mom. We rode our bikes. On our way home, my friend dropped some of his change in front of the bus stop. When we stopped to pick up his change, two guys at the bus stop told us to get away from their money. My friend said that it was his money and started to pick it up. When he bent over to pick it up, one of the guys kick him and his bike in to the street. When my friend tried to pick his bike up, one guy pulled his shirt up and showed a gun that was in his pants. He told my friend to leave *his* bike alone to. But it was really my friend's bike. My friend ran across the street and almost got hit by a motorcycle and a car. I rode away to. My friend's mom gets real worried a lot and doesn't let him go many places on

his own. So we told her that his bike was stolen while we were playing video games in the store.

P.S. Do you think I should tell my mom what really happened?

My Response to the Class

My immediate response to the "P.S." question was that he should let his mom know the real story. I also seized the "teachable moment" offered by the letter. The incident was a great opportunity to stress that although we may not always understand or agree with the restrictions placed on us by our parents, there is usually a very good reason for those restrictions.

Anonymous Student

Dear Officer ———,

Can you give me some advice on how to help my brother. I'm worried about him because he smokes cigarettes. He used to only smoke when he was with his friends, but he never inhaled the smoke. Now he even smokes when his friends are not around. He also smokes the regular way now **(by inhaling the smoke).**

He used to sneak cigarettes out of my mom's purse. He would only take one cigarette at a time so my mom wouldn't notice that they were missing. My mom said that she is going to stop smoking. In class you said that people who become addicted to drugs sometimes steal so they can get the drugs, when they don't have money to by them. Well, I think that my brother is addicted to nicotine. If my mom stops smoking, I'm afraid that he might start stealing cigarettes from the store. I don't want to tell you his name because you were his officer last year, when he was in the fifth grade. You can read this to the class and tell me what to do. Thank you for helping me.

Sincerely,
Your Student

Chapter 20
Responding to the "Toughies"

A significant portion of each presentation is set aside, during which the students are encouraged to ask additional questions that are not necessarily related to the lesson. I have found this to be the most effective way of addressing the issues that are of the most concern to the students. I try to be as open and honest, as is appropriately possible, in responding to each question. However, there are the occasional "toughies." These are the questions to which there are no simple or apparent answers. The "toughies" usually come from one of two sources. Either they come from a student who sincerely hopes that you will have an adequate answer, to justify the level of respect and credibility that you have achieved with them, or the question comes from a student who hopes that you will not have an adequate answer, thus greatly diminishing the level of respect and credibility that you have achieved with the other students, hence, justifying his or her own lack of respect for you.

Regardless of the source, if handled properly, "toughies" can provide great "teachable moments" as well as create significant opportunities to provide valuable information to the students regarding serious issues of concern. I often feel as though I have "fallen short," when responding to the "toughies." However, I give it my best shot. In this chapter, I have included some of the more common "toughies" that I have received over the years as well as my best efforts to respond to them. **Please remember that these are elementary-level children.**

Toughie #1

These are a few variations of the same questions.

If alcohol is so bad for people and it can damage your stomach, liver, and heart, then why do some adults drink anyway?

Sometimes my mom drinks wine and my dad drinks beer. Will they become alcoholics?

Note

I adhere to three major rules when responding to questions from my students. These are that I don't lie to them, I try to avoid being critical of their parents, and if I don't know the answer, I tell them that I don't know the answer.

Response

I simply emphasize the following points.

As adults, your parents can legally purchase alcoholic beverages. Some day each of you will reach the age when you can legally purchase alcoholic beverages. Should you choose not to drink, be confident about that decision, and assertive of your right to be a non-drinker. Should you choose to drink, hopefully you will also choose to do so responsibly (i.e., not drinking while operating a vehicle, not drinking to the point of impairment, and respecting the right of others to be non-drinkers). If and when you make the decision to become a drinker, it should be because you choose to drink, not because of peer pressure or a desire to fit in with others.

Finally, there is a difference in using something and abusing something.* Abuse means to misuse or mistreat something or someone. If your mom has a single glass of wine on occasion, she is not abusing alcohol. However, for a variety of reasons, American society has chosen to make it illegal for children to consume alcohol. Therefore, drinking alcohol as a juvenile could constitute abuse.

Toughie #2

Dear Officer Babb.

I have tried every thing that I can think of to get my mom to stop smoking cigarettes, but she still smokes them. I have told her about all of the health consequences that we learned about in school. I also added up how much money she spends every year on cigarettes. I even wrote her the letter telling her why I want her to stop smoking. I 'm worried about her. I don't want her to get sick or die. What should I do now?

Note

I was surprised to find the issue of parental smoking to be such a prevalent and traumatic concern among my young students. I have had students come to me in tears over the issue of a parent who smokes. However, if you consider the issue from a child's perspective, it is not too difficult to understand why they become so concerned.

Children of today are bombarded in school as well as in the media about the harmful effects of tobacco use. They see the famous black lung photo in their text books and continually hear of famous smokers who have died of cancer. So when one of the most important people in the child's life smokes, it shouldn't be difficult to understand why a child becomes so concerned. The following is my "last resort" advice to students. This advice comes once all other advice has failed and when the child's concerns have reached the point of affecting them emotionally and academically.

Response

At this point in their life, your parents are well aware of the possible consequences of smoking. Therefore, to continue lecturing them regarding those consequences will probably have a minimal effect. At this point you have done all that you can do to let them know that you are concerned about them. As intelligent and informed adults, they have made a conscious decision to continue smoking and to risk the possible consequences of their decision. Their smoking is no longer your responsibility. Your responsibility now is to respect the decision that they have made. If the smoke bothers you physically, then they will hopefully respect your rights enough to not smoke when they are near you, meaning of course that you may have to occasionally relocate when they light up.

Toughie #3

Dear Officer Babb,
    Why is marijuana illegal? My dad says that marijuana should not be illegal because you can't get addicted to it and it doesn't cause cancer. He also says that it's safer than alcohol, because you can still drive OK after you smoke it. I think the only reason that it's illegal is because people can make a lot of money, and the government doesn't like for some people to make a lot of money. My dad says that marijuana is better for you than tobacco. When do you think that marijuana will be made legal? Why do you and the teachers keep lying about marijuana being bad for you?
Not Signed

Note: Gee! I wonder from whom this attitude came.

    The big dilemma here was finding a way to respond without being critical of Dad. We had covered the possible consequences of using marijuana, during previous lessons; therefore, anything more than a brief review did not seem practical. In recent years, society has become more tolerant of marijuana use. Many employment applications that once read "Have you ever experimented with any illegal drug?" now read "With the exception of marijuana, have you ever experimented with any illegal drug?" Some police departments now separate marijuana from other illegal drugs, when addressing the issue of drug use, during the application process.
    Many children no longer see marijuana use as a serious issue. Upon finding cocaine or heroin in a suspect's pocket, it is not unusual to find marijuana in the one of the other pockets. It has been said that you can judge a

person by the kind of friends that they keep. How then should we judge marijuana? Marijuana is often referred to as a "Gateway" drug. This is due to the tendency of marijuana to lead its users to other, harder drugs.

My Response

I decided to take the fair and impartial route, by having a class discussion on the matter. Following the discussion, we took an informal poll. While many of the students did not see marijuana as a serious threat, only one student felt that it should be legalized.

Toughie #4

Dear Officer Babb,
    My son ——— is in one of your classes. I was informed that he will be participating in an essay assignment regarding his pledge to stay drug free. I understand that several of the students will be chosen to read their essay during their graduation. While I certainly do not have a problem with the students pledging to be drug free, I do have concerns regarding the competitive aspect of the essay assignment (i.e., selecting certain essays for special recognition).
    My husband and I feel strongly that every effort should be made to limit the exposure that our children have to competition. By exposing a child to competition, we also expose that child to rejection. I am sure that you will agree that our children will receive enough exposure as they enter the postgraduate world. We would greatly appreciate your further consideration on the competitive aspect of the essay assignment.

Note

There is a growing movement within the academic community to limit, if not completely eliminate, competition in schools. This growing movement has prompted some school districts to eliminate recognition for special student achievement, such as valedictorian and other special honors that students have spent much of their young lives striving toward.

At one particular school, I was informed that the principal did not want the students to have a DARE graduation. The reason given was that they did not want to risk upsetting the parents of those students who were not recognized for special achievement. In addition, the principal did not think it was fair to recognize the students who had excelled, over the students who had not, including those who had never even put forth a serious effort. Of course this was also a school which requested that I not involve the parents in the program. The following is my response to this parent's letter.

Response

Dear Mrs. ———,

Thank you very much for your recent letter as well as the suggestions that you offered regarding the essay assignment. Please accept my praise for the active interest that you have shown in the program, as well as in your child's academic experience. I wish more parents would take the same level of interest in their child's education. I appreciate the candor of your comments. I certainly hope that the same appreciation will be reciprocated on behalf of my response.

Our job as parents and as educators is to help prepare our children to function in a "real world" environment. In that "real world" environment, they will be exposed to competition and rejection on a daily basis. Therefore, it is vital that our children acquire the coping skills that are necessary to function successfully in such an environment. Please consider the following realistic scenario.

Upon graduating from college, your child goes on his or her first dozen job interviews. Of course he is only one of fifty people who are also applying for the same job opening. Following the first six rejections, which is highly probable, he begins to feel the stress. Having little prior exposure to competition and rejection, he lacks the coping skills necessary to cope with such feelings. How then does he or she cope? It has been my experience that many of these people end up putting a needle in their vein or a bullet through their head. As cruel and imperfect as this world may be, it cannot be improved by pretending that its realities do not exist.

In reality, the world does include competition. It is this reality that helps us to acquire the additional life skills necessary to cope with the other harsh realities of life. I believe that competition encourages children to set goals and inspires them to become the very best that they can be, in order to achieve those goals. In the process of becoming the very best that they can be, they learn to deal with victory, defeat, acceptance, and rejection. Competition helps our children to learn self-discipline, integrity, and teamwork. Competition has also enabled us to realize advances in medicine and technology. Without competition, aspects of our society will simply stagnate and die. As much as we want to shield our children from the harsh realities of life, by doing so, I feel that we are doing them a grave disservice.

I feel certain that you would much rather have your child's first exposure to these pressures occur in the safety of a structured classroom environment, rather than in the unpredictable environment of a real world scenario. The possible consequences of "trial and error" in the classroom are far less severe than the possible consequences of "trial and error" in the real world. When our children make a mistake in the classroom, we can be there to cushion their fall. However, when they make a mistake in the real world, we will most likely not be around. While I may not have sold you on my philosophy, I do appreciate having the opportunity to share it with you. . . .

Sincerely,
J.A. Babb

Note

Although I did not win this parent completely over to my way of thinking, we did reach an acceptable compromise regarding the essay assignment as well as other aspects of the program. The results of our compromise were so positive that it has been permanently implemented in my program. It is amazing what can be accomplished when parents and educators work together.

Toughie #5

Dear Officer Babb,

In our lesson about inhalants, you said that we shouldn't use things the wrong way because it might hurt us. Well, my mom breathes in air from helium balloons sometimes to make us laugh. It makes her talk funny. I told her what we learned about people who smell things to get high. She said that it was okay to smell helium because it won't hurt you. She said that teachers just tell us things like that to scare us, so we won't do it. She still won't let us do it though because we're too little.

Response

I have yet to discover an adequate way of responding to this one.
Do as she says, not as she does???

Note

All of the effort and dedication of those who educate our children is virtually useless if what they learn in school is not reinforced in the home.

Responding to the "toughies" offers unique opportunities for the instructor. It affords the instructor an opportunity to address the actual issues of concern to the students. The "toughies" also provide an excellent opportunity for instructors to enhance their own credibility, as well as the rapport they have with the students. The "golden rule," when responding to the "toughies," is to never bluff the students when you do not know the answer to the question that you have been asked. This will cause an instant loss of credibility with the students. If you do not have an answer, say so. When I have no answer to a "toughie," I simply respond by saying, "You know, I honestly do not know the answer to that question. Why don't we talk about it? What do you think?"

Children love for adults to take an interest in what they think or how they feel about a particular topic. They are always willing to give adults their own opinions. Believe me! Children have already figured out that adults do not have all of the answers. Therefore, they are very impressed when an adult actually admits this. I like to say "From the mouth of babes often comes good advice." Some of the best advice that I offer is advice that I acquired simply by listening to the children.

Chapter 21
Who Made Me an Expert?

(Answer: Your children!)

It was several years ago that I first felt compelled to write a book for parents on the subject of communicating with their children. Upon approaching my wife (a veteran schoolteacher with a natural gift for working with young children) with the idea, I was stunned by her response. "Why write a book that no one is going to buy?" she asked. In an attempt to better understand this apparent lack of support, I encouraged her, somewhat graphically, to explain. She continued, "You have to be an expert before people will buy your book or even listen to what you have to say. You're not even a parent, so why should they listen to what you have to say?" Realizing that she had a valid point, I retired to a warm bath to tend my wounds.

Several weeks later, I was sitting in the "roll-call room" awaiting my patrol assignment for the shift. Prior to the end of roll-call, a nicely dressed young man entered the room. He was a college student wishing to participate in the civilian "ride-along" program. This occurs when a civilian is allowed to ride with a police officer for an entire shift. I agreed to let him ride with me.

The first couple of hours were filled with excitement. Toward the middle of the shift, things began to calm down, so I suggested that we grab dinner while we had the opportunity. He agreed and asked if he could bring a tape recorder along, in order to record my responses to some questions that he intended to ask.

Although his tape recorder refused to function correctly, the interview continued. Following a barrage of questions regarding crime and police work, I decided to conduct an interview of my own. The interview went like this:

Me: "So, why do you have such an interest in crime and police work?"

Student: "Actually, I am more interested in crime itself."

Me: "Oh, why crime?"

Student: "Well, I am working on my doctorate and I need this information for my thesis."

Me: "Why write a book that no one is going to buy?"

Student: "Why do you think that no one will buy it?"

Me: "I thought you had to be an expert before people will buy your book."

Student: "Well, it does help if you are considered to be an expert."

Me: "So what exposure have you had to crime that qualifies you as an expert on the subject?"

Student: "Well, this 'ride-along' is the only practical experience that I've had."

Me: "Let me see if I understand this. You spend eight hours riding with a veteran police officer who has dealt with crime on a day-to-day basis for years. During that eight-hour shift, you ask the officer for his opinion regarding crime. Then you write a book, as an expert on the subject of crime, and people flock to the stores to buy it."

Student: "Hopefully! The book, along with my doctorate, will cause me to be considered an expert on the subject of crime."

Me: "Darn, look at the time!"

I spend approximately fifty hours each week with children of all ages, ethnicities, academic abilities, and socioeconomic backgrounds. I teach them in class, eat with them during lunch, play with them during recess, and attend dance recitals, ball games, and swim parties. I also see, firsthand, the pressures that these children are exposed to when they are away from their parents. With all of this experience, I am nowhere close to being an expert. I realize this now more than ever, as I begin raising my first child. Children of today are far different from the children of yesterday. They are more sophisticated; they have different values, beliefs, goals, and interests. They face far different and more complex pressures than children of the past. The children of today must learn a variety of new roles in order to function in a more complex and ever-changing society.

It is more important now than it has ever been for parents to "keep up with the changing times." Unlike many of our parents, we must learn to *communicate with,* rather than *just talk to,* our children. The traditional line, "I was once a kid too, you know," will no longer work. Parents of today cannot possibly know what it is like to be a child today. Contemporary parenting has become a partnership, and the key ingredient needed for success is communication. Our children will help us guide them, if we will just listen to them and hear their needs and concerns. One of the greatest mistakes that a parent can make is to assume that our children are just like we were.

In the following pages, I will attempt to offer my own observations, which are based on the success that I have had in communicating with my students. I hope it will be accepted in the sincere spirit that it was intended.

Chapter 22
The Search for Understanding

One day I was approached by a parent who had recently discovered through a friend of her son that her child was experiencing some significant personal problems. She was perplexed over the fact that she always seemed to find out about the problems her son was experiencing, through his friends. She could not understand why her son chose to confide his personal problems in his friends, rather than come to her or his father for help. The answer to this phenomenon, simply stated, is because they are parents. As a parent, as far as your child is concerned, you do not understand their dilemma. Therefore you are not considered a credible source of advice and support. **(Don't write this off yet. It will eventually make sense, I hope.)**

Often when a child comes to a parent with a problem, he is looking less for advice than he is for understanding. He would much rather speak to someone who can relate to what he is going through rather than have someone give him advice who has no clue as to what he is going through. Your child's peers are either experiencing or have experienced what your child is going through. They can relate to the feelings, the emotions, and the pressures that your child is experiencing. Although the parent may be more qualified to give responsible guidance and support, in the mind of your child, his peers are a more credible source of information and support.

Consider the following two conversations, the first of which occurred between a mother and her child, and the second between her child and myself. To help you better understand these conversations, I will take a moment to set up the scenario.

It is a warm breezy afternoon and I am visiting with a parent who is concerned about the recent changes in her son's attitude toward school. Although David, her teenage son, normally has a positive attitude toward school, lately his attitude toward school has become somewhat negative. Although his mother had made several attempts to discover what the problem was, she had not been successful in getting him to open up. She mentioned that she had become concerned after learning that this new attitude was beginning to affect his grades, especially in his math classes. She further stated that David had always done well in his math-related subjects; however, recently his grades had suffered. As we are speaking, David returns home from school. Sitting quietly at the kitchen table, I witnessed the following conversation between David and his mother.

    Mom: "Oh! You're home."
        David: "Hey! You're quick, Mom."
        Mom: "What's wrong with you?"
        David: "Nothing . . . Hey, Officer Babb."
        Me: "What's up, buddy?"
        David: "Just recovering from a day of school."
        Mom: "What's with this sudden attitude you have toward school?"
        David: "I just don't like school."
        Mom: "You love school!"
        David: "Not anymore!"
        Mom: "Why not?"
        David: "Because I just don't, Okay, Mom?"

Mom: "No, it is not okay. I want to know why you don't like school anymore."
David: "Because I'm stupid, Mom."
Mom: "Oh, my gosh! Why do you think you are stupid?"
David: "Because I am, Mom. I'm stupid! You have a stupid son. Get used to it, Mom."
Mom: "You are not stupid and I don't want to hear you say that again. Is that understood?"
David: "Sure thing, Mom" (as he disappears into his bedroom).

Well, David did obey his mother's order. He never again said that he was stupid, in her presence. Although his mother succeeded in stopping David from saying that he was stupid, **did that solve his problem?** Did we even discover what his problems were?

David re-emerged from his bedroom with a football and invited me to go outside to throw the ball with him. Upon accepting his invitation, we exited to the back yard. This will be the setting for the second conversation that I will share with you.

Me: "So, do you really think that you're stupid?"
David: "Yeah, I guess."
Me: "That's cool!"
David: "What's cool? That I am stupid?"
Me: "No, that you think you are stupid."
David: "Why do you say that?"
Me: "I'm glad to find out that I am not the only person who felt stupid in school."
David: "You felt stupid in school?"
Me: "I sure did!"
David: "Why did you feel stupid?"
Me: "Algebra!"
David: "You're not good in algebra?"

Me: "I am now, but didn't use to be."

David: "So, why did you feel stupid?"

Me: "I had always done very well in math-related subjects, until algebra came along. I had always been in accelerated math classes. So, when I had algebra, I was placed in an accelerated class. However, for some reason I just couldn't catch on to it as quickly as the other students in the class. I was finally moved to a regular algebra class."

David: "So, how did you become good in algebra?"

Me: "Once I was in a regular paced algebra class, I began to understand the subject a lot better. Actually, I eventually had one of the highest averages in the class. Then I began to realize that all the time that I thought I was stupid, I was actually just a normal student. There is nothing wrong with being normal. I would rather think of myself as being normal than as being stupid. Anyway, I decided to make algebra my main priority. I was determined to become an expert on the subject."

David: "Did you ever make it back into the accelerated class?"

Me: "No, I never did make it back into that class. But at least I knew that I was not stupid. In addition, I realized that I was the only person, in the regular algebra class, who had ever been in accelerated classes. So, not only was I not stupid; I was still above average."

David: "That makes sense."

Me: "So, which subject makes you feel stupid?"

David: "Geometry! Do away with geometry, and school would be okay."

BINGO! Now we have discovered the actual problem. It was not that David disliked school; rather, it was that he was having problems with geometry. The sudden insecurities that David was having toward school were a manifestation of the problems that he was having in one particular subject. You may recall that it was not until he discovered that I could somewhat relate to his situation, that David began to take an active interest in what information I had to offer. Upon attaining this newfound level of credibility, David was willing to share his problem with me.

Once a child senses that the parent understands or can relate to their problem, an intimate bond is created between the child and that parent. This works to enhance future attempts to communicate with one another as well. I honestly believe that children would much rather consult their parents or other respected role models, regarding such troubling matters. However, they feel that since their parents cannot relate to their situation, they could not possibly understand their problems. Hence, the child's parents are not considered to be a credible source of advice and assistance.

Chapter 23
The Hidden Meaning

> When a child tells of an event, it is sometimes helpful to respond, not to the event itself, but to the feelings around it.
>
> —Dr. Haim G. Ginott,
> *Between Parent and Child**

Although Dr. Ginott was addressing a slightly different scenario than I am about to share with you, the fact remains that we often need to look beyond the statements, questions, and actions of our children to achieve an understanding of their real concerns. I can best illustrate this premise by sharing with you an experience that I had at one particular school.

Since it is of particular significance in this story, I will take a moment to recreate the setting. This particular school is located in a small, affluent community. Its students are among the brightest; their parents are among the most involved and devoted with whom I have worked. The performance and behavior of its students help to affirm the high academic standards by which this school functions. However, as with most things in our society, this success has come at a price, a very high price in my

---

*Haim G. Ginott, *Between Parent and Child* (New York: Avon Books, 1956), p. 31.

opinion. While these children are adequately prepared to compete in the business world, they are somewhat sheltered from many of the harsh social realities to which they will be exposed in the real world (i.e., gangs, drugs, etc.). Hence, in the opinion of many, these particular children are poorly prepared to cope with these additional social pressures that will be brought upon them throughout their lives. It is this precious naivity, that will also place these children "at risk" of becoming future victims. Now that the setting has been established, I will continue with the story.

While its attendance area includes mostly upper income homes, there is one small lower income apartment complex that falls within the jurisdiction of this affluent school. Its weekly rates tend to cater to a more transient clientele. It was from this apartment complex that "Little Johnny" came. Johnny was a quiet and mysterious young man, about whom little was known. Lacking many of the polished social skills and the stylish attire, which were customary for the students of this school, Johnny immediately stood out among his classmates.

When he first came to the school, Johnny received a lot of attention from the other students. Rather than being repelled by his peculiarity, many of the students seemed to be drawn, out of curiosity, toward him. During my first recess and lunch with these children, it appeared as though Johnny was very popular with the students. Anytime that I observed him, there always seemed to be a small crowd around Johnny, made up primarily of boys.

Upon returning to the school for our next lesson, I discovered the "Question Box" in each classroom to contain twice the normal amount of entries. I further discovered that the additional entries all pertained to the same topic: Johnny. For some reason Johnny had begun telling the other students that he was a member of a gang, and that he could have the gang beat anyone up who messed with him. He evidently went on to describe some of the dangerous activities in which he and his gang participated.

Upon returning to the school, I was approached by several who requested a private conference in order to tell me about Johnny. I was finally approached by a teacher who asked that I do something about "the Johnny situation." She complained that her class was continually being disrupted by students wanting to speak to her privately regarding their concerns about Johnny.

Johnny ate lunch alone that day. Following lunch, Johnny took his regular position on a playground bench during recess. However, this time he was all alone. For some reason, the other students were avoiding him. I spent recess on the bench with Johnny, discussing the rumors that I had heard regarding his membership in a gang. During our conversation, Johnny continued to insist that he was in a gang. However, as he continued to share his story with me, it became obvious that it was fabricated. While it was obvious that Johnny had some prior exposure to gangs, his story was not consistent with the gang situation in this particular community. This realization only enhanced my own curiosity. Why, if he was not in a gang, did Johnny want others to believe that he was involved with one? Certainly it was not an attempt to impress his classmates so that he would be even more popular. If this was his motive, it was having the opposite effect.

At the request of the school counselor, as well as his teacher, Johnny and I had a private conference, on the following morning. During the conference, I informed Johnny that I knew he was not really in a gang. He responded by saying, "I know; I just want everyone to think that I am so they will be afraid of me." When asked why he wanted them to be afraid of him, Johnny responded, "So they won't mess with me." Johnny went on to explain that where he came from, if you were associated with a gang, no one messed with you. Thus creating this environment in which others feared him was a learned survival skill. It definitely worked in this case. The other students steered clear of him, once he identified himself a gang member.

I knew these students to be intelligent, responsible, and compassionate people. I explained to Johnny that he was in a different environment from that to which he had grown accustomed, that he did not have to worry about these kids messing with him. I knew that they would reach out to him if he gave them a chance.

Johnny and I devised a plan that would enable him to recant his gang story and still "save face" in the eyes of his classmates. With tears in his eyes, Johnny confessed that he did not know how to make friends with other people. I replied, "You make friends with them the same way that you just made friends with me, by being honest and by being yourself."

Unfortunately, this story did not have a happy ending. After giving Johnny my word that we would work together, my efforts were undermined. Another officer was brought in later that day to talk to Johnny. Not being privy to the "hidden meaning," they decided to treat the symptom rather than the illness. The officer chose to use intimidation tactics, which may have worked in some cases. However, in this case, they did more damage than good. That was the last time that I saw "Little Johnny." For whatever reason, his family abruptly packed up and left town. As one of his teachers put it, "It really worked out for the best. He will now be someone else's problem.

He's no longer our problem." If she only knew how much of "our problem" it will really be.

Revisiting my earlier point, it is sometimes necessary to look beyond the surface and past the mere symptoms, to find the root cause and to "treat the illness." Before we leave this particular subject, I would like to share one more brief scenario with you. This scenario is perhaps a little more common than the prior scenario.

A parent of one of my students had become concerned about her daughter's sudden interest in the subject of divorce. Over a period of one week, her daughter had asked the following questions of her: "Do you love Daddy? Why did you marry Daddy? When you and Daddy get a divorce, where will I go?" Upon discovering that their daughter had asked the same questions of her father, they became concerned. The parents eventually voiced their concerns to the school counselor, who ultimately requested that I attend the parent meeting. After hearing their concerns, the "hidden meaning" behind their daughter's concerns began to emerge.

Several of their daughter's classmates had parents who were going through divorce. One of her classmates was living with her mom, another was with her father, while a third had been sent to live with her grandparents. Each child had expressed a sadness over the absence of one or more of their parents in their life. Divorce had become so common in her life that she was beginning to accept it as a natural stage in marriage.

On the surface, their daughter seemed to be concerned about divorce. However, her real concern was over what would happen to her if and when her parents got a divorce. Her questions were an effort to deal with the insecurities that she was feeling. They were a way of seeking reassurance that she would not have to experience the loss of a parent. With this knowledge, her parents now understood the "hidden meaning" behind their daughter's questions and were able to help reassure their daughter.

After proofreading this particular chapter, a friend asked, "How can you find the hidden meaning?" I certainly do not want to imply that there will always be a hidden meaning, although the "hidden meaning syndrome" tends to be much more prevalent with younger children.

When a young child asks me a question, I will first answer the question and then follow up with my a question of my own, such as: "What made you ask that question?" or "What made you think about that?" This not only helps you discover if there is a hidden meaning, but it also lets the child know that you have taken a sincere interest in his or her concerns.

Chapter 24
A Child's Feelings; A Child's Right

> A child's feelings must be taken seriously, even though the situation itself is not very serious.
> —Dr. Haim G. Ginott,
> *Between Parent and Child**

Can you recall how many times as a child, you went to a parent regarding a life-changing and earth-shattering dilemma, only to have your concerns belittled and discounted as being childish or ridiculous? Chances are that you can. It was done to us as kids and whether intentional or unintentional, we do it as adults. At a stage in life when peer pressure is at its strongest and "fitting in" is of the highest priority, the most insignificant matter to an adult can become a major dilemma for a child.

Consider the following scenario: I have two fourth-grade girls who have been friends since birth. They attended the same school, participated in the same sports, clubs, and Brownie troop, saw movies together, spent many nights together, and accompanied each other on occasional family outings. Their names began with the same two letters, therefore, they were usually placed in the same group or team, when based on alphabetical

---

*Haim G. Ginott, *Between Parent and Child* (New York: Avon Books, 1956), p. 23.

order. They were inseparable buddies, until the fourth grade, when fate dealt them the cruelest of blows. Their fourth grade teacher organized the class into cooperative learning groups. You guessed it; they were placed in separate groups. To witness this event, you would think that their lives had come to an end. As incredible as it may seem, Tiffany and Angela did manage to overcome this horrible tragedy. However, it would only be a few weeks before the next tragedy was to occur. This tragedy, however, would take its toll on these two precious girls.

During the next few weeks, Angela became friends with another girl, who had been assigned to her group. This new girl was affectionately nicknamed T.F.S. (The Friend Stealer) by Tiffany. I was eating lunch with Tiffany, when she learned that Angela had accepted an invitation to spend the night with T.F.S., her new "best friend." Unfortunately, the Life Flight (medi-vac) was not available; therefore, a standard ambulance would have to do, were Tiffany to be in need of transportation to the hospital. Tiffany was devastated. From the nurse's office, she called her mom and asked to go home early. Mom, understandably irritated, having been called from a business luncheon, advised Tiffany that she would have to remain in school until it let out. Then her mom agreed to pick her up from school, rather than have her ride the same bus home as Angela.

As she had promised, Tiffany's mother picked her up from school that day. After hearing the details of Tiffany's dilemma, her mom could not help but react to the humor of the situation. Of course Tiffany became upset by her mom's reaction. After realizing how seriously Tiffany was taking the matter, her mother informed her that the entire matter was ridiculous and that she was handling it in a childish manner. After brief, verbal combat, the conversation ended with Tiffany's mom saying, "Don't worry, you will get over it."

Actually, her mom was right on two, of the three, counts. Tiffany will eventually "get over it." She was handling the situation in a childish manner; but, then again, she is a child. However, her third assessment is relative. What appeared to be ridiculous to her mom was very real to Tiffany. Her feelings needed to be respected and accepted as being legitimate. A child's concerns are reason for concern simply because the child says that they are, regardless of how ridiculous we may deem the circumstances to be, in which they occur. Those feelings need to be respected and addressed as if they were our own feelings.

Chapter 25
Is Your Child "at Risk"?

It is always disturbing to me when **ethnicity** or **economic status** is used to determine whether or not a child is "at risk." In contemporary society every child is "at risk," regardless of who they are, or where they live.

I have had the privilege of working in several of the nation's most exemplary schools. One such school (I will delete the name, for sake of discretion) is a small school that is located in a relatively affluent community. Aside from having teachers who go beyond dedication, and a leader who is a true diplomat, what makes this school truly special is the unselfish support and involvement of the parents.

One day while visiting this school, I was engaged in conversation by a parent whose child attended the school. After praising the need for gang and drug abuse resistance programs such as the D.A.R.E. program, the parent expressed concern that too much academic time was being sacrificed for the program. She went on to express a sentiment that I have heard all too often. I call it the **"not my kid syndrome."** The parent asked if I thought that the children of (*school) really need this program. "After all," she continued, "it's not like our school has the same problems as some of the other schools . . ." (She went on to name several other schools within the district.)

I first responded by pointing out that the students

attending those schools, that she identified as having problems, all feed their students into the same middle school that her child will eventually attend. Hence, that middle school inherits the "problems" of those other schools. However, the children from the "problem" schools have been previously exposed to that pressure environment. Therefore, they have been able to develop the additional coping skills that are necessary to function successfully in that environment. Her child, on the other hand, coming from a more sheltered academic environment, will enter middle school having never been exposed to this new pressure environment. Lacking these additional coping skills, that wonderful, innocent, and dedicated honor student, now becomes an "at risk child."

In addition, her child will patronize the same convenience stores and the same malls and will attend the same school sporting events as those other "problem" children. It happens! I have seen it! No child is immune!

Every child is an "At Risk" child.

FYI: This particular parent went on to be very supportive of the program, especially for middle-school students.

Chapter 26
Jason's Story

How a Good Kid Became a Victim

Jason was a good kid. He could easily be described as "a parent's dream." He was an excellent student who voluntarily devoted many hours to his studies. He loved school and he loved learning. He was active in many extracurricular activities, including Scouts, swim team, roller hockey, and several school activities. While he enjoyed many activities, the one activity to which he most looked forward was their frequent family gatherings where his many achievements usually dominated the topics of discussion. He enjoyed cooking out and just being with his close-knit family.

Jason lived in a small, relatively affluent community. He attended a small public school that had the atmosphere of an exclusive private school. He had attended this particular school since the first grade; therefore, it was the only school that he had ever really known.

Unfortunately, Jason's family became victims in a troubled economy and were forced to relocate their home to a more affordable community. Their new home was located within the boundaries of a very large school district. Jason's new school had a student population that was about three times larger than that of his former school. Living relatively close to the school, Jason chose to walk to and from school each day rather than have his mother drive him, as she had previously done. Having adjusted well to the move, Jason was looking forward to the first day at his new school.

Jason's first day at school went well, as did the following three weeks. As was customary for Jason, he remained active in school activities. Being involved in a variety of school clubs, Jason was often among the first students to arrive in the morning and among the last students to leave the school each day.

One afternoon Jason stayed after school for a club meeting. He had remained after the meeting for just a couple of minutes to finish organizing his things. When he began walking through the hall, toward his normal exit, he noticed that he was quite literally the last student around.

As he exited the building, Jason took his usual shortcut to the sidewalk, which ran parallel to the school, by cutting across the school lawn. As he angled his foot route to intersect the sidewalk, he noticed a small group of boys farther down the sidewalk who were walking in the same direction. Although he did not recognize the boys, he immediately recognized the colored clothing that they were wearing. The boys' attire identified them as members of a local gang.

As he neared the sidewalk, Jason realized that if he continued his current pace, he would intersect the sidewalk just ahead of the gang members. Not wanting to draw attention to himself, Jason slowed his pace so that he would fall in behind the gang. However, as he slowed his pace, he noticed that they did the same. Jason felt a sudden hot flash throughout his body as his chest began to tighten. He slowed his pace once more, hoping that the gang had not focused their attention on him. However, once again, the gang slowed with him. Feeling that it would be premature, as well as foolish, to run, he entered the sidewalk ahead of them.

As he continued to walk, Jason could sense that the gang was getting closer. Slowing his pace, in hopes that the group would just go around him, Jason began silently praying to himself. Suddenly, two boys appeared on each side of Jason, as if the group had split in order pass him. However, rather than pass Jason, they continued to walk right along side of him.

As he felt the impact of a hand on his left shoulder, Jason heard one of the boys speak to him.

"Hey, man! Where you headed?"

"I'm just going home."

"Long day at school?" another boy asked.

"Yes, I'm in the computer club."

"You must be new here?"

"Yes, I've only been here for a few weeks."

"Didn't anyone tell you that it's not safe to be out alone around here, especially if you're new?"

"Ya, you have to watch out for the gangs," chuckled one of the boys.

"Don't worry, you're covered as long as we are around. In the future, you need to find some friends to walk with though."

"Okay," replied Jason.

As they approached a small bridge, which was located midway between the school and Jason's home, the boys suddenly stopped.

"Well, this is where we get off. You're on your own from here," the apparent ringleader said.

"Okay, thanks!" Jason replied.

"Yeah, man; we'll see you around."

Feeling as though he had just survived a close call, Jason continued his walk home.

The following day, not wanting to push his luck, Jason exited the school from a different door. Upon exiting the building, Jason was relieved to find no sight of the gang in the area. As he approached the opposite end of the school building, the gang suddenly appeared from beside the school. Once again, Jason could feel his chest tighten.

"Walking home alone again?" the ringleader asked.

Jason did not reply.

"Man, we can't be here every day to protect you."

Once again the gang split, placing Jason in the middle as they continued to walk with him. As they had on the previous day, the gang stopped on the bridge and left Jason on his own.

During the next week, no matter which exit that Jason took, the gang always appeared. As in the past, they would always leave him at the bridge. However, they had always been very polite to Jason and never caused him any harm.

On the following Friday, Jason was excited about the family gathering that had been planned for the weekend. Although his day was going well, he was eagerly awaiting the end of the school day. Several relatives had come to town for the family gathering, and Jason was looking forward to spending time with them once he returned home from school.

As he cut across the school lawn, Jason noticed that the gang was nowhere to be seen. With cautious optimism, he continued walking toward the far end of the school where the gang had intercepted him on several prior occasions. However, as he approached the end of the building, there was no gang to meet him. This made Jason experience a wonderful sense of relief. For the first time in over a week, Jason felt secure.

Assuming that the gang had finally lost interest in him, Jason continued his walk home. As he neared the bridge, Jason noticed several figures emerge from underneath the bridge and look in his direction.

After briefly conversing with one another, all but one of the figures walked back underneath the bridge. As he approached the bridge, Jason recognized the remaining figure as the gang's ringleader. Realizing that taking such evasive actions as crossing the street or running would be foolish at this point, Jason continued without altering his route.

Once they made eye contact, the gang leader began to speak.

"Jason! What's up, buddy?"

"Nothing, I'm just trying to get home."

"Now what did we tell you about walking alone?"

"Yes, I was in a hurry today and didn't have time to wait."

"Well, come over here for a minute; I have something to show you under the bridge."

"No, I really need to get home. My family is waiting on me."

"Oh, come on; you can spare a few minutes for your buddies."

The gang leader placed his arm around Jason's neck and gently guided him underneath the bridge. Once under the bridge, Jason observed the remainder of the gang. As he looked around, he could see cigarette butts and empty beer cans littering the area.

As the ringleader motioned, the gang members surrounded Jason. At this point Jason was terrified. As he felt his heart beating, he listened to the words from the ringleader.

"Listen up!"

"For the last week, we have been letting you walk home with us, so no one would mess with you."

"Yeah, man, we've been protecting you," added another gang member.

"We've taken good care of you and now you owe us."

"It's time for you to take care of us."

Jason was too frightened to respond.

"Listen, man, just chill out and listen to what we want you to do."

"We want you to go to this food mart and get us a twelve-pack of beer."

The ringleader explained to Jason how he could go about stealing the beer. He then advised Jason that once he completed this assignment, that he would no longer owe the gang. Jason was then warned that if he tried to go home without completing his assignment, they would eventually get him. As he turned to leave, Jason was given a final shove by one of the gang members. Once he reached the street, Jason could hear a voice from below: "Don't you make us have to come looking for you."

On his way to the store, Jason tried and tried to come up with a solution for dealing with the situation. However, he could not think of any way out, other than to follow the gang's instructions and get them out of his life for good.

Jason entered the store and began walking toward the beer section. However, as he neared the alcoholic beverages, he noticed that the clerk was observing him in one of the mirrors. Jason bypassed the beer and walked up another aisle. He knew that what he was about to do was wrong; however, he saw this as his best and quickest way out of this situation. With the clerk watching him,

Jason knew that he stood little chance of making it out of the store with the beer.

As he continued up the aisle toward the front of the store, Jason saw his opportunity. There in front of him was a beer display, which was made up of twelve-packs. Without hesitation, he grabbed a pack of beer and ran toward the exit. As he exited the store, he ran past one of his school coaches, who happened to be entering the store.

Jason ran as fast as he could and did not stop until he reached the bridge. Out of breath and sweating, Jason went below the bridge and handed the beer to the ringleader.

"Here it is. Can I go now?"

"Yeah, man; get out of here."

As he turned to leave, one of the gang members grabbed him by the shirt and slung him around against the concrete wall of the bridge.

Once again, Jason found himself surrounded by the gang.

"Hey, man; this beer is hot. We don't drink hot beer."

As the gang members took turns assaulting him, Jason went down to the ground, hoping that the beating would stop. Following several more kicks to his face, chest, and ribs, the beating stopped.

As Jason lay on the ground, beaten and bleeding, the gang members began pouring cans of the warm beer over his small body. As the gang members left him lying there, Jason began wondering how something like this could have happened to someone like him.

With the help of therapy, Jason fully recovered from his physical injuries within one year. His family has moved away from the big city to a much smaller community. They feel somewhat safer in this small community;

however, they have vowed to never again let their guard down.

Jason was a good kid. No one ever dreamed that something like this could have happened to him. Jason was never taught to deal with such a situation. Therefore, Jason became a victim of not only the gang, but of those who either refused or failed to see the need to prepare him.

It is no longer enough to "just say no" and to want to do the right thing. We must now teach our children how to say "no" and how to do the right thing. We must give them the basic skills to deal with an increasingly complex society. We all have a stake in their future.

Chapter 27
Fulfilling Your Child's Needs

> It has by now been sufficiently demonstrated that the human being has as part of his intrinsic construction, not only physiological needs, but also truly psychological ones. They may be considered as deficiencies which must be optimally fulfilled by the environment...
> —Abraham H. Maslow,
> *Toward a Psychology of Being**

I often receive questions from parents regarding the existence or absence of specific factors that I felt could cause a child to become "at risk." While there are a variety of factors that could lead a child to become "at risk" only those factors that I consider to be the greatest determinant on whether or not a child becomes "at risk," will be addressed in this chapter. These factors are those that I found to be deficient in the lives of many troubled children and that were abundantly present in the lives of other children.

In his famous hierarchy of needs, Abraham Maslow (1970) assigns basic human needs to five categories. He further proposed that the more basic of human needs must be satisfied before it is possible to satisfy the higher level needs. While the latter has been challenged, I would like

*Abraham H. Maslow, *Toward a Psychology of Being* (New York: Van Nostrand Reinhold, 1968), p. 152.

to focus on the basic human needs that Maslow has identified. Among the basic needs identified by Maslow are:

Self-actualization needs—realizing one's full potential as a productive, creative person.
Esteem needs—self-esteem; esteem from friends.
Belongingness and love needs—acceptance, friendship, and companionship.
Safety and security needs
Physiological needs—food, water, and shelter.

In addition to the needs that Maslow has identified, I would like to add some needs which I feel are essential for the emotional and psychological health of every child. These additional needs are:

Recognition—a need to be recognized for one's accomplishments.
Identity—achieving an awareness of the intrinsic qualities, which create the uniqueness that distinguishes one from others.
Consistency—In a fast-paced and ever-changing world, it is crucial that a child have some consistencies in his or her life. For a child, this can include family, friends, pets, and a routine. With the daily barrage of pressures, challenges, and surprises, it is nice to occasionally know what is coming around the corner.
Structure—It is no secret that children need structure in their lives. However, it may come as a surprise to some that children actually prefer structure in their life. This is evidenced by the fact that a growing number of youth gangs have now published handbooks for their juvenile

members. These handbooks attempt to establish strict standards regarding conduct, discipline, dress code, recognized hand signs, graffiti, etc.

These basic needs are essential for the emotional and psychological development and well-being of every child. It is imperative that these needs be satisfied through appropriate sources. When these needs are not met, children will often turn to other sources in an effort to have these needs satisfied. Often those other sources may involve gang involvement or drug use.

As much as we may dislike gangs, they do serve an important purpose in the lives of their members. A gang satisfies a child's need for acceptance and belongingness, safety and security, self-esteem, recognition, identity, and many more needs. Of course many of these needs can also be satisfied by membership in a baseball or soccer league. This is one reason I so strongly recommend that children be encouraged to participate in team or group activities. So many of their needs can be satisfied through interacting with their teammates. It is far better that their additional needs be met by fellow teammates rather than fellow gang members.

The best of parents and the closest of families cannot fulfill all of a child's needs. Therefore, it is imperative that appropriate, alternative sources be available to help satisfy these unmet needs. It is when these needs are not being met that children turn to gangs, drugs, and other inappropriate sources, in an effort to have those needs met. By ensuring that your child's needs are being met through appropriate means, you greatly decrease the likelihood that you child will ever become involved with drugs, gangs, and other unsafe or illegal activities.

Chapter 28
Divorce: From a Child's Perspective

Through their letters, as well as through personal counseling, children have enabled me to view divorce from a different perspective: their own. Through the hearts and tears of children, I have been able to witness first hand the disruptive effect that divorce can have on a child's emotional, psychological, and in some cases physical wellbeing. While the innocence of my own childhood was stolen through abuse and a bitter, never-ending divorce, I do not claim to be an expert on either the subject of abuse or divorce. Since divorce has a unique effect on each person it touches, there can be no single expert on the general subject of divorce.

It would take much more than a single chapter to cover the topic of divorce and the impact it has on the lives of all who are affected. Therefore, this chapter will cover divorce from two perspectives: the children's and my own. The following information will include aspects of divorce that I have observed to be of greatest concern to my students.

The Good Divorce

In her book, *The Good Divorce: Keeping Your Family Together When Your Marriage Comes Apart,* Dr. C. R. Ahrons defines a good divorce as "one in which both the adults and children emerge at least as emotionally well as they were before the divorce." In a good or successful divorce, involving children, the family still functions as a family. The mother and father are still responsible for the physical, emotional, and psychological development of their children. Of course both parents remain financially responsible as well. Although the family structure may have changed from that of a nuclear family to that of a "binuclear family,"* each parent remains responsible for fulfilling his or her role as a parent. Just because a couple may have been unsuccessful in marriage, does not mean that they cannot be successful in divorce. As long as each parent has a mutually well-defined role as parent, there should be no reason that the former couple cannot work together to foster the lifelong investment in the future of their child.

When Should the Children Be Told?

Timing is important. Once parents have made the

---

*The concept of binuclear family was developed by Dr. C. R. Ahrons in her landmark longitudinal study of family relationships after divorce. *The Good Divorce,* (New York: Harper Collins, 1994.)

"It's every kid's right to know what's happening in their life"—*The Kids' Book of Divorce,* Eric Rofes, editor. (New York: Vintage Books, 1982), p. 23.

decision to separate or divorce, the children should be told. The most common question I receive from children who have just been told of a pending divorce is, **"What's going to happen to me?"** This is an extremely insecure time for a child. His or her own future is at stake here. If he or she is told secondhand or long after the decision has been made, they feel as though they have been left out of the decision-making process. If the child is told in a timely manner, he is reassured that his parents have taken his future into consideration. A child needs to be reassured that both parents will remain an active part of his life.

As one of my students once complained, "I feel shut out. They act like they are the only ones who will be affected by this divorce." Fear of the unknown, especially when it involves the future of the child and his family, can be traumatizing to a child. Although the child does not need to know the intimate details of the pending divorce, they do need to at least achieve an understanding of what is happening, as well as how it is going to affect them.

How Should a Child Be Told?

Perhaps the most essential of all phases in a divorce is how the children will be told. Whenever multiple children are involved, it may be best to tell them all at the same time. This is preferred for several reasons. If children are told together, rather than separately, they will receive a degree of comfort in knowing that they are not going through it alone. In addition, when told jointly, the children may be able to assist each other in coping with the situation.

It is also preferred that parents jointly tell the children of the pending divorce or separation. This can be beneficial to the parents as well as the children. For the parents, it reduces the possibility that one parent will be able to assign blame to the other parent or only tell one side of the story. This also lends credibility to the parents, in the eyes of the children.

In addition to enhancing credibility, this method also reassures the children that they are being figured into the equation.

Although some experts may disagree, parents should choose the illness over the symptoms, when explaining the reason for the divorce. Your child does not need to know the graphic details of an extramarital affair. The affair is merely a symptom of a much larger problem. Aside from initiating an assortment of emotional responses in the child, this may cause the other parent to begin airing more dirty laundry in an effort to justify the affair, or to enhance their own standing with the child. However, a parent should never lie to the child. If asked a direct question, give an honest answer. How a child is told of the divorce can greatly affect the degree of success that child will have in coping with the situation. Remember! "Honesty is the best policy."

What Does Your Child Need to Know?

One of the dilemmas faced by divorcing parents is deciding just exactly what information should be shared with their children. This judgment can only be made by the parents who are involved. However, there are some basics that need to be shared with the children involved. These are:

1. Reaffirm your love and devotion to your children.
2. Let the children know why their parents are separating or divorcing.
3. Let them know where each parent will live.
4. Let them know where the children will be living.
5. Reassure them that both will remain their parents and will take an active role in their upbringing.
6. Let them know how visitations will work.
7. Make sure the children realize that the divorce is not their fault.
8. Make them aware of any challenges or difficult decisions that may be ahead.

These are only a few of the issues that need to be addressed in the event of a divorce or separation. Obviously each situation is unique and may dictate that additional issues be addressed. The less you leave to the child's imagination, the better he or she will handle the situation.

Assigning Blame

Whether overt or covert, consciously or subconsciously, there is often an attempt by one or both parents to win the allegiance of the children. A parent will sometimes employ a variety of methods to persuade the child that the other parent is to blame for the failure of the marriage. As Dr. Edward Teyber states in his book *Helping Children Cope With Divorce:* "Often this blame is assigned by inappropriately providing children with specific details of adult infidelities and sexual relationships."

This practice is not in the best interest of the child

and should be avoided. Your child has a right to love and respect each parent. Just because one spouse may have failed at being a husband or a wife does not mean that they will fail at being a parent as well. The child will be the ultimate judge in these matters.

There appears to be a correlation between a child's maturity and the manner in which they assign blame for marital breakup. It has been my own observation that children below the third-grade level are more likely to place the blame with themselves. Younger children are more likely to wonder what they have done to cause their parents to break up. Typically, first and second grade children are more prone to feel as though they have been rejected by the departing parent.

The older children (third-grade level and up) appear more likely to assign blame to a particular parent. The blame is usually assigned to the parent who leaves or to the parent who has had an extramarital affair. Every step should be taken to let the child know that the marital problems of their parents are not in any way their fault.

Parentification

In a healthy two-parent family, the role of the parent and the child are well defined. Following a divorce, children of single-parent families will often take on additional responsibilities in order to help fill the void left by the departing parent. In addition to relinquishing some of their adult responsibilities, the single parent will sometimes come to rely upon the child to help meet other personal needs. It is when the child begins to take too many of the adult responsibilities and attempts to satisfy emotional needs of the single parent that problems begin to arise. In such situations, previously well-defined roles between adult and child become clouded. In a sense, a role reversal occurs. This role reversal is sometimes referred to as **parentification.**

A good example of a parentified child can be found in chapter 7 (**Letters from Anonymous**) letter # 6. You will recall that the letter had been written by a student who wanted to apologize for being late for school. The reason given for her tardiness was that she had to get her brothers ready for school, drop them off at the bus stop, and prepare breakfast for her mother. This student was clearly performing tasks that would normally be the responsibility of her parent.

The effects of having been parentified become evident in the child's adulthood. As Dr. E. Teyber states, in his book *Helping Children Cope with Divorce* (p. 170):

> Parentified children grow up to feel overly responsible for others, afraid of depending on others, and guilty about having their own needs met. Because the basic model of relationships they have learned is taking care of others, parentified children often reenact the roles of provider or rescuer in subsequent relationships.

It is not unusual in their adult relationships for parentified children to be drawn to others who have problems, such as alcohol or other substance abuse. Since they are caretakers by nature, they feel comfortable in these dysfunctional relationships. These children, who are praised in childhood as being so mature and responsible, have difficulty becoming adults.

There is certainly nothing wrong with giving a child additional responsibilities. However, it is important to ensure that there is still a clear distinction between the role of the parent and that of the child. It is important that a child be allowed to have a childhood, in order for that same child to become a healthy, productive, responsible, and secure adult.

The Do's and the Don'ts

The Do's

- Let the children know exactly what is expected to happen, before it happens. The fewer surprises the better, for everyone involved. Fear of the unknown is especially strong with children who are facing a pending divorce. Letting them know what to expect lessens their feeling of powerlessness and enhances their ability to cope.
- Settle into a routine as soon as possible, regarding visitations and other divorce-related changes. Contrary to what some may think, children actually prefer having a routine.
- During the first year of separation, it is especially important for the absentee parent to spend as much time as possible with the children. This will help quell the fear of abandonment many younger children experience following a divorce.
- Allow your child to remain close to the other parent. Remember, in most cases, the problems are between you and your spouse. Do not allow bitter feelings to result in your child being deprived of a relationship with both parents.
- Let your child know, in no uncertain terms, that the marriage has or will be ended and that the

divorce is permanent. If children feel that there is a chance their parents may once again be reunited, they will postpone accepting the divorce. This will prolong the stress for everyone involved.
- Communicate with your child's teachers, friends, your former spouse, and most important of all, your child. Aside from just being a good practice, it will also help you to monitor how your child is coping with the divorce.

The Don'ts

- Do not use your child to spy on your former spouse.
- Do not use your child as a bargaining tool or weapon when dealing with your former spouse.
- Try to avoid talking your former spouse down while in the presence of the children.
- Never tell or imply that your child is responsible for your marital problems. If many of the conflicts, during your marriage, center around the children, that does not indicate that your child is the problem. Those conflicts, regarding the children, are merely a symptom of a greater problem.
- Do not forget that your child still needs you.
- Do not pressure your child into addressing a stepparent as "Mom" or "Dad." Let them do this on their own, and in their own time. The ultimate compliment, for a stepparent, is for a child to assign one of these titles on his or her own. Just give the child time. If it happens, that is great. If it doesn't happen, "join the club." Having a stepchild who does not refer to you as "Mom" or "Dad" does not mean that they do not accept you as a parent,

especially with older children. The terms "Mom" and "Dad" are defined differently by each child. Give that child love, respect, friendship, and affection, and you will be that child's definition of "Mom" or "Dad."

Regardless of the circumstances, divorce is traumatic for all who are involved. For both parents, it is the end of lifelong dreams and the beginning of "starting over." For children, it is the realization of an unthinkable nightmare. As difficult as it is for the parents, who have a degree of control over the situation, it is far more difficult for the children, who have no control. Regardless of the circumstances, it is imperative that the children be the main priority. Parents who were unable to work together in marriage must learn to work together in divorce. The parental accord or discord experienced by children, will impact relationships far into the future. Those relationships that will be affected in the future will not necessarily be limited to the immediate family. As parents of today, we are laying the groundwork for how our children will conduct their future relationships. Therefore it is imperative that we accomplish, in divorce, what we were unable to accomplish in marriage. Your child needs both of you. As Dr. E. Teyber states in his book *Helping Children Cope with Divorce:*
"The shared act of conception entitles children to both a mother and a father."

Chapter 29
Helpful Hints for Parents

In this chapter, I will include some helpful hints for parents. While these helpful hints cannot guarantee that your child will never become a victim of drugs or gangs, they can help decrease the likelihood that such a tragedy will occur. The following are just a few suggestions that parents may want to consider.

Encourage your child to be active. Encourage your child to become involved in extracurricular school and social activities. Preferably, these should include some team or group activities.

Attend your child's extracurricular activities—i.e., games, concerts, etc.

Occupy your child's free time. Give them additional responsibilities.

Spend time with your children. Set aside time for family activities, as well as time for one-on-one activities in which multiple children are involved. In addition to the overall family relationship, a parent should have a special relationship with each child, being careful not to show signs of favoritism.

Set limits for your child at an early age. Children need and want structure in their life; however, waiting until your child is in his or her teens to set limits will meet with limited success.

Establish consequences and follow through

with their enforcement. Set clear boundaries and guidelines for your child. Once you have made them aware of the possible consequences of violating the boundaries, follow through with their enforcement. I cannot emphasize enough the importance of following through with the enforcement of consequences.

Be fair and honor deals or commitments made to your child. If you give your word to your child, **honor it** and make it clear that you expect the same level of integrity from your child.

Begin developing good communication with your child at an early age. This involves listening as well as talking. Take an interest in your child's concerns, ambitions, interests, social life, etc. Keep up with their social life (friends, boyfriends, girlfriends, co-workers, peers, etc.). When children have a problem and need someone to talk to, they prefer talking to someone who is already aware of the situation and its main characters. This way they do not have to spend a hour catching you up on the history of the problem.

Know your child's friends, co-workers, workers and others with whom they associate. Have your child invite friends to participate in some activities. Whenever possible, become acquainted with the parents of your child's friends.

Participate in your child's education. Attend parent meetings and school activities. Help your child with homework and projects. However, this does not mean that you should do the work for them.

Become involved in your community. Attend civic associations meetings and become aware of what is going on in your community school.

Discourage your child from associating with known gang members.

Encourage your child to avoid known gang hangouts. Do not allow you child to wear gang-related clothing. Your child's school and the local police department are excellent sources of related information.

Do not allow your child to write gang graffiti or display gang gestures.

Do not allow your child to stay out late and roam the streets unsupervised.

Be aware of any drug or gang problems in your community. Again, schools and local police departments are excellent sources for related information.

Encourage your children to keep up with current events. Encourage them to watch the news. This exposes them to what is going on in the real world. It also provides an excellent opportunity to discuss issues of concern to you and your child. In addition, this creates an opportunity to enhance the rapport between you and your child.

Do not just assume that your child knows you love him or her. Continually reinforce your love.

Praise your child. *Sadly, I have been advised that I need to elaborate this point. There are many way to praise your child. There is nothing wrong with having a collection of "stock responses." Some responses might be "Good job," "Excellent work," "Way to go," "All right," "Fantastic," "Awesome," "Outstanding," "That was a great try," "Good work," "Much better." It is a good idea to vary the "praise" phrases that you use. While praising your child is important, it should not prevent the use of constructive criticism and other corrective measures. Your child depends on you to teach him or her values, appropriate behaviors, and other life skills.

Watch for warning signs:

- sudden changes in
  - —academic performance—attire—friends
  - —attitude toward authority—personality—interests
- Truancy
- Sudden interest in martial arts (out of the blue)
- Sudden interest in weapons

As I previously indicated, there is no system of parenting that can guarantee your child will never become a victim of drugs, gangs, or some other tragedy. These days a parent can do everything right and still have problems. Hopefully, in addition to these helpful hints, with a lot of love, dedicated parenting, understanding, and an open mind, you can drastically reduce the chances that your child will ever become "at risk." The fact that you have taken the time to read this text is a good indicator that you will be successful in your parenting endeavors.

Chapter 30
An Afterthought

You may have noticed that a majority of these letters and requests for help appear to have come from females. It has been my own experience that approximately **90 percent** of the contributions to the **"Question Box"** are of female origin, a startling statistic with serious implications for society. This statistic may lead a person of ignorance or who is oblivious to believe that males have either fewer problems, a greater capacity for handling their own problems, or that males just eat less quiche than females. Excusing my own ignorance, I will attempt to explain.

It is no shocking revelation that a majority of violent crimes are committed by males. It is also no secret that men have traditionally chosen more aggressive means of expressing themselves or of releasing stress than have women. While a variety of theories have been offered to explain this phenomenon, it continues to be a debatable matter (and will continue to be, long after this book has been relegated to use as a leveling device for that unstable piece of furniture, or to raise that slide projector another inch on the screen).

As you may have figured, I am prepared to offer my own theory, which may be the theory of others as well, on this matter. I believe that the origins of this difference of expression can be found in the process by which males and females are socialized. I realize that this part is not earthshaking news. In traditional as well as contemporary society, females are encouraged to be open and expressive of their feelings. It is acceptable for a female to cry when she is upset, or to seek counseling and advice from a friend, when there is a problem. Males, on the other hand, are encouraged to be strong and independent. It is not as socially acceptable for males to cry, show weakness, or to be expressive of their feelings, although we are beginning to experience a change in the latter. Again, I realize that this is not earthshaking news. Please bear with me; I'm nearing the point that I wish to make.

I have read many of the self-help books for women. (I have been unable to locate a great number of self-help books for men. I'm still looking for the book entitled *Men Who Love Women, and the Women Who Hate Them*.) As I read about all of these emotions that are experienced by women, I found that I could relate to them. **NOW FOR MY POINT!!!**

Rather than differentiating between "**female** emotions" and "**male** emotions," we should see them as "**human** emotions." As human beings, we must have an outlet for expressing these emotions. If held in, over a period of time, these emotions will eventually manifest themselves in other ways, such as violent and aggressive behavior. These pent-up emotions are sometimes manifested in the form of health problems, such as ulcers, heart attacks, drug abuse, etc. Coincidentally, males appear to dominate the market on the latter issues as well. **I look forward to a day when the contents of the "Question Box" will include a more equal number of questions and letters from male and female students.** With one foot remaining on my "soap box," I will tell one quick story to conclude my point:

One day, while observing a coed class of fifth graders

in the gym, I witnessed an argument between a girl and a boy. It actually became quite heated. The argument concluded with the girl walking away in tears and going to a group of friends for comfort. The boy, on the other hand, slammed a plastic hockey stick into a trash can, causing it to briefly go airborne, walked to a far corner of the gym, and sat by himself along the wall. This is not an entirely unusual problem-solving scenario with children or adults. My intent here is not to condone the problem-solving technique of the boy, nor is it to necessarily endorse that of the girl. Rather my point is that these two children are only ten years old. Regarding the difference in behavior between boy and girl: How much of the behavior is of primal influence and how much is of social influence? To what degree are we, as a society, our own worst enemy? I will leave the questions to the experts. Our children are being raped, robbed, assaulted, and murdered by each other. Hopefully we will find the answers soon before we deplete our greatest national resource: our children.

FYI: One week later, as I entered the school building, I was advised by other students that the boy and girl were now "going out." Wherever "out" might be, for fifth graders.

Chapter 31
To the Critics

(And There Will Be Many)

As my experience has shown, there will be those critics who will question the appropriateness of the degree to which I become involved with my students and their families. There will be those who will question my motives as well as those who will irresponsibly speculate as to my possible ulterior motives. To these critics I have now grown accustomed. However, I will briefly attempt to address some of those issues that are sure to follow.

Issue #1:

Claims have often been made that officers such as myself are on a covert mission to recruit children as spies in an effort to catch parents, as well as their own peers who may be guilty of misdeeds.

Response:

Aside from its asinine nature, this claim is simply not true. Were this to be the case, it would be counterproductive to the expressed mission of indiviudals such as myself. It often takes weeks, in some cases months, of concentrated effort to dispel the stigma and stereotypes that come with being a police officer. Once this has been done, and the officer has achieved the status of a sincere friend and confidant in the eyes of the children, it would be irresponsible and outright foolish for the officer to engage in behavior or to take any actions that would jeopardize his rapport with the children. The first time an officer arrests a child's parent, or is unduly harsh with a child (especially if the arrest was based on information shared in confidence by a student), this rapport is blown. Once compromised, this rapport is virtually impossible to fully regain. Once the children perceive you as a source of intimidation, you have been rendered ineffective. As a general rule, it should only be in extreme circumstances involving the safety and well-being of a child that an officer should take such action. I have addressed more than twenty-five thousand students and have never had cause to effect an arrest.

A nightmarish scenario would be for a child to approach an officer with a kilo of cocaine, saying "I found this in my dad's drawer. I don't like when he uses it because he gets real mean. I don't want you to get him in trouble, but can you make him stop?"

Issue #2:

Some will claim that I become too involved in the personal lives and problems of my students or their families.

Response:

I may be inclined to agree with this issue of criticism. However, when you observe that a student who is rarely absent suddenly begins missing school; a student who routinely has a hearty appetite suddenly starts skipping lunch; a student who is normally very outgoing suddenly becomes introverted; a student who is normally well dressed suddenly takes on a disheveled appearance, approaches you in tears asking for help and refuses to be directed to anyone else for help, let me ask my critics what they would have me do.

It is important to keep in mind that these instructors (officers) are in the classroom for an expressed purpose. They are there by virtue of their special ability to work with and motivate young minds and to share the knowledge which they have acquired from years of firsthand experience on the streets, as well as that which has been gained from years of specialized training. Their overt mission is to assist these children in acquiring the coping skills which are necessary to make healthy and responsible decisions, and to enable them to resist the pressures to become involved with gangs and drugs. Perhaps most important of all, they are there as an additional resource in a child's support system, a system of support in which the primary contributors should be the parents and family.

It is my sincere belief that the key to success in preparing our children to be successful, productive, and well-adjusted members of society lies with the family unit. The day upon which the family is secure, not only in its makeup but in fulfilling its functions as well, my job will no longer be necessary. Until that day comes, I will rely on a cliché that I have heard somewhere in my past.

Although I am unsure of the exact wording or who is to be credited for it, here it is to the best of my knowledge: "It is far better to light a candle than it is to curse the dark."

Chapter 32
My Next Project

(Depending on How Well This Project Goes)

Upon entering a school one morning, I heard a commotion in the hallway. Directing my attention toward the lunchroom entrance, I observed that the commotion was being caused by an emotionally distraught little boy. Surrounded by two teachers and a cafeteria worker, the third grader was wailing away, with tears streaming down his cheeks and neck. Upon approaching the scene, I was advised by one of the teachers that the little boy had just returned to school following a prolonged absence, which was due to the loss of two family members.

Seeking comfort and reassurance, the little boy reached out to one of the teachers, as if he wanted to be held. I watched in shock as the child was gently repelled by the teacher. My shock was then compounded as I watched the other teacher take a step back, in order to avoid contact with the child. As I went down on one knee, the child enveloped me with a hug. Feeling some of the child's tears flowing down the back of my neck, I looked up, in indescribable anger, at the two teachers.

However, as I looked into the eyes of each teacher, I could tell that they were desperately fighting back their tears. My anger soon turned to confusion. I could sense the repressed passion that they felt for the child and what he was going through. At an age when stability and consistency are so vital, for emotional and psychological development, this child had just lost two of the most consistent people in his life. He probably looked forward to returning to school, in order to be with his teachers and classmates, the few remaining consistencies in his young life. I could not understand why the teachers had reacted the way that they had.

Throughout the day, each of the teachers approached me in an effort to explain their actions or inactions. I also received several friendly warnings, regarding the possible consequences of having any physical contact with the students.

Later that day I was approached by another faculty member, who advised me that another parent had become concerned upon hearing that I had allowed the child to hug me. Upon sharing this experience with the two teachers, one responded, "Welcome to the teaching profession. Teach but don't touch."

Since this incident, I have been inundated with some incredible horror stories about teachers who dared to care about their students. Some of these stories will hopefully be shared in my next book.

References

Ahrons, Constance R. *The Good Divorce: Keeping Your Family Together When Your Marriage Comes Apart.* New York: Harper Collins Publishers, 1994.

Benjamin, Ludy T., Jr., J. Roy Hopkins, and Jack R. Nation. *Psychology,* 2nd edition. New York: Macmillan Publishing Co., 1990.

DARE America. Official DARE officer's curriculum for elementary schools (updated version—1994).

Ginott, Haim G. *Between Parent and Child.* New York: Avon Books, 1956.

Maslow, Abraham H. *Toward a Psychology of Being,* 2nd edition. New York: Van Nostrand Reinhold, 1968.

Teyber, Edward. *Helping Children Cope with Divorce.* New York: Lexington Books, 1992.

The Unit at Fayerweather Street School. Edited by Eric E. Rofes. *The Kids' Book of Divorce: By, for & about Kids.* New York: Vintage Books, 1982.